BOLDT YACHT HOUSE - Fern Isla

It was on Sunday, July 23, 1893 that 41-year old *George Charles Boldt* first arrived at Ale: wife *Louise*, who had been vacationing there for several weeks with their children, 14 year sister, *Louise Clover*. Impressed with the beauty of the Thousand Islands, and the beautif again the following summer, and again in 1895. It was then that they obtained *Hart Island* and changed the name to *Heart Island*. The wood frame cottage that was on the island served as their summer home when at the Thousand Islands. *Heart Island* is only one of over 1,600 in this picturesque paradise.

George C. Boldt was the owner of the *Bellevue* and *Stratford* hotels in Philadelphia, Pennsylvania. The *Stratford Hotel* was torn down in 1902 and the *Bellevue-Stratford Hotel* was built on that site. Mr. Boldt was also the proprietor of the *Waldorf* and *Astoria* hotel's which were on 33rd and 34th Street in New York City. Both were torn down in 1929 and the *Empire State Building* is now on that site.

GEORGE CHARLES BOLDT SR. and *JR.* – *LOUISE CLOVER* and *LOUISE AUGUSTA KEHRER BOLDT*

Five-acre Heart Island was too small for George C. Boldt's ambitious mind. So he set his sights in a westerly direction from his 5 acre *Heart Island* estate and on January 31, 1897 he gave $900.00 to *Mr. Charles W. Crossmon* and his wife *Mary E. Crossmon*. This purchase was for a portion of Fern Island, which was just 2,200 feet away from *Heart Island*. By June 18th of that same year *Mr. Boldt* would gain more property on Fern Island when he gave $250.00 to the *Westminister Park Association*. This section had a dock and a small building on it and used as a freight house. An additional part of Fern Island was owned by *Mr. Gilbert T. Rafferty*, which *Mr. Boldt* purchased from him on April 14, 1899. The amount paid was $500.00. These 3 parcels gave *Mr. Boldt* ownership of the entire island.

Fern Island is off Wellesley Island and is in a bay on the northwest side of the main channel of the St. Lawrence River and directly across from the Village of Alexandria Bay, New York. *Mr. Boldt* would begin building a large new yacht house on this land in the fall of 1899.

The land *George C. Boldt* was purchasing was not to be just for investment only, but to be built upon and developed for his use. Brothers *George W.* and *William D. Hewitt*, architectural firm from Philadelphia, Pennsylvania, were *George C. Boldt's* favored architects who designed the *Boldt Yacht House*. They designed the *"shingle style"* structure with the conscious use of native construction material such as granite, pine, and cedar shingles to blend the massive yacht house with its rustic island surroundings, and was a further reflection of the *Hewitts'* sensitivity to contemporary architectural trends. The yacht house would become a highly eclectic structure, which exhibits a wealth of stylistic detail. The *Hewitt's* also designed *Boldt Castle*, the *Hennery*, and the *Power-House*, all on *Heart Island*. In addition they would also design the *Bellevue-Stratford Hotel* for *Mr. Boldt*.

MUD CREEK MARSH - FERN ISLAND

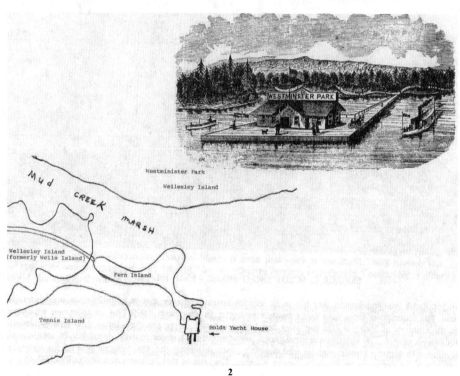

2

THE *BOLDT YACHT HOUSE* - THE CIRCULAR TOWER ON THE LEFT WAS THE RESIDENCE OF THE CARETAKER, *CAPTAIN GEORGE WAGNER*. THE SMALL STRUCTURE ON THE RIGHT WOULD BE REMOVED FOR A NEW ADDITION.

The foundation for the new yacht house was begun in November 1899 and stands on a mortared fieldstone foundation. The circular tower, office/storage wing, and caretaker's residence are wood frame structures, while the 3 services bays, which housed *Mr. Boldt's* growing fleet of boats, are framed with a system of prefabricated, lattice-braced steel truss members. These prefabricated sections were built in New York City and sent in sections by barge to *Fern Island* to be assembled.

The *Boldt Yacht House* was completed in the summer of 1900, and is 160 feet long and 115 feet broad and covers only 1 acre of *Fern Island*. The structure is a steel frame, wooden building, more than 50 feet high. The entire building is sheathed in weathered shingles. In its range of structural forms, design motifs, and materials, the *Boldt Yacht House* is an eclectic tour de'force unsurpassed in the estate architecture of the *St. Lawrence River Region*. Visually, the horizontal emphasis achieved by the rambling mass of the structure is balanced by the vertical thrust created by the steep gables, towers, spires, chimneys, and cupola, which dominate each elevation.

The *"shingle style"* of architecture with its towers, spires and steep-pitched gables, gives the *Boldt Yacht House* a sophisticated design. The huge doors on the second and third bays opened in sections almost to the peak, allowing for the tall mast of *Mr. Boldt's* steam yachts *Louise* and *Presto* to enter the structure. The *Boldt Yacht House* contained a machine shop, with electric power, storage and sleeping rooms.

In May 1905, *Mr. Delancey Porter* was contracted to build an addition to *Mr. Boldt's* yacht house on *Fern Island*. This fourth service bay was used for *Mr. Boldt's* beautiful 104 foot houseboat, *LaDuchesse*.

BOLDT YACHT HOUSE WITH THE HOUSEBOAT *LADUCHESSE* AND THE STEAM YACHT *LOUISE*. ABOVE THE NEW STEEL FRAME ADDITION BEING CONSTRUCTED ON THE RIGHT. BELOW, NOTE THE UNFINISHED NEW ADDITION ON THE RIGHT.

In the picture above are men standing on top of the new steel framing to the *Boldt Yacht House*. Two of the men were *Harold* and *Floyd Perry*, who also worked at building *Boldt Castle* on *Heart Island*. The picture was taken by their mother *Emma Perry* while on her way to deliver lunch by boat to her two sons. Both boys were born and raised in Clayton, New York

THE COMPLETED ADDITION ON THE RIGHT. BELOW *BOLDT YACHT HOUSE* ON *FERN ISLAND* CAN BE SEEN AT THE LEFT. *THE PEACOCK YACHT HOUSE* ON THE RIGHT. THE VILLAGE OF *ALEXANDRIA BAY, NY* IS IN THE BACKGROUND. *TENNIS ISLAND* AND *WELLESLEY ISLAND* ARE IN THE FOREGROUND. THE WATERWAY IS REFERRED TO AS *"THE BOLDT CANAL."*

ABOVE THE *BOLDT YACHT HOUSE* AS SEEN FROM THE *BOLDT CHANNEL.* THE *PEACOCK YACHT HOUSE* CAN BE SEEN AT THE RIGHT AND IS NO LONGER IN EXISTENCE. BELOW THE *BOLDT YACHT HOUSE* IS IN THE LOWER CENTER AND *MR. BOLDT'S* HOUSEBOAT *LADUCHESSE* IS MOORED NEXT TO IT. *BOLDT CASTLE* ON *HEART ISLAND* IS IN THE CENTER AT THE LEFT. THE VILLAGE OF *ALEXANDRIA BAY* IS AT THE TOP

The *Boldt Yacht House* is a massive eclectic building, which actually combines 4 separate structural elements in a single functional entity. These elements include a circular tower containing reception rooms; a central group of 3 large slips or service bays for yachts; a combination office and storage wing with its crenellated tower; and a large caretaker's residence. The building's orientation is such that its 3 service bays open to the east.

Included inside the 3 service bays there is a mechanical system with overhead traveling crane on dual tracks, 7 pairs of screw jacks for raising vessels out of the water for service, and a steel expansion sleeve to the cupola to facilitate interior operation of the steam and gasoline engines of *Mr. Boldt's* boats. A sense of the building's massive scale is conveyed by the central yacht bay, which measures 160 feet in length and 46 feet in height above the waterline.

The circular tower to the left of the yacht house was the residence of the caretaker, *Captain George Wagner*. This structure features reception rooms characterized by decorative oak ceilings, moldings and wainscoting, ornate carved stair balusters and newel post, and fireplaces of cut and fitted stone.

SHOWN BELOW IS THE CARETAKER RESIDENCE OF THE *BOLDT YACHT HOUSE*. THE LEFT PICTURE LOOKS WEST WITH *WELLESLEY ISLAND* IN THE BACKGROUND. THE RIGHT PICTURE LOOKS EAST AND SHOWS *BOLDT CASTLE* ON *HEART ISLAND* IN THE BACKGROUND

HIGH ATOP THE *BOLDT YACHT HOUSE* IS THIS CHARMING CUPOLA. INSIDE THE CUPOLA IS A STEEL SLEEVE THAT COULD BE LOWERED DOWN OVER THE SMOKE STACK OF THE STEAM BOATS INSIDE THEREBY ACTING AS A CHIMNEY. VISITING THE *BOLDT YACHT HOUSE* WERE *FLORENCE E. WAGONER* ON THE LEFT AND *CHRISTINE PHILLIPS THOMPSON*, WIFE OF *CHARLES THOMPSON*, ELECTRICAL ENGINEER FOR *MR. BOLDT*

AT THE *BOLDT YACHT HOUSE* WERE *FLORENCE E. WAGONER* ON THE LEFT AND HER GOOD FRIEND *CHRISTINE PHILLIPS THOMPSON*, WIFE OF *CHARLES THOMPSON*, ELECTRICAL ENGINEER FOR *MR. BOLDT*. IN THE BACKGROUND IS *BOLDT CASTLE* ON *HEART ISLAND*. THE BOAT IS BELIEVED TO BE THE *BABY FROST* WHICH BELONGED TO THE *WAGONER* FAMILY

George C. Boldt had lavished more than $50,000.00 on building his yacht house. The building soon became a seat of yacht-oriented resort life for *Mr. Boldt* and his wealthy peers. The yacht house must have given *Mr. Boldt* great pleasure and enjoyment. As a builder and boater he took great pride and interest in the maintenance of his vast fleet of vessels. Many men were employed by him to operate and maintain the various watercrafts.

George C. Boldt died at 6:00am on Tuesday December 5, 1916. His death occurred in his apartment on the ninth floor of the *Waldorf-Astoria Hotel* in New York City. His estate of about $15 million dollars was equally divided between his son *George C. Boldt Jr.,* and his daughter, *Louise Clover Boldt Miles*, wife of *Alfred Graham Miles*. *Mr. Boldt* was 65 years old.

Mr. Francis S. Hutchins, personal attorney for *Mr. Boldt*, and of the law firm of *Baldwin & Hutchins*, 27 Pine Street, New York City, filed an appraisal of the watercraft owned by *George C. Boldt*. He also had an appraisal done of the electrical supplies, machinery and tools that where at the *Boldt Yacht House*. The affidavit of appraisal was notarized on July 14, 1917 by *Mr. Charles Putnam* of Jefferson County. *Mr. Frederick W. Adams* did the appraisal, which reads;

"Frederick W. Adams, being duly sworn, deposes and says: I reside at Alexandria Bay, New York, and am a duly licensed engineer, and a practical ship builder, having been in the ship building business, for over 10 years, during which time, I worked on the building and reconstructing of ships, also bought and sold ships and their accessories, including machinery and tools, and during the said period of years, I bought electrical supplies, machinery and tools, such as used in steam yachts and launches, and by reason of such experience, I am thoroughly familiar with the values of electrical supplies, machinery and tools, as set forth in the inventory hereto attached.

"That during the month of June 1917, I personally examined and inspected for the purpose of appraising all the electrical supplies, machinery and tools, said to have belonged to the decedent herein, at the time of his death, December 5, 1916, and have appraised the same as of that date, as more fully set forth in the inventory hereto attached, and am of the opinion that if the said electrical supplies, machinery and tools, had been offered for sale on the said day of death of this decedent, they would not have realized more than $4,406.44, which was the fair market value thereof on the said 5th day of December 1916."

The appraisal was submitted to the Surrogate's Court, New York County, in the matter of the appraisal under the transfer tax law of the estate of *George C. Boldt*, deceased.

JUNE 1917 INVENTORY OF ELECTRICAL SUPPLIES AND STORED IN THE *BOLDT YACHT HOUSE* AT *ALEXANDRIA BAY, NEW YORK* BELONGING TO THE ESTATE OF *GEORGE C. BOLDT, DECEASED.*

RESEARCHERS NOTE: THE TWO ITEMS MARKED WITH AN ASTERIX ARE NOT COMPUTED CORRECTLY ON THE ORIGINAL INVOICE.

ELECTRICAL SUPPLIES

50 - 1/2" Conduits	@ .24	$12.00
50 - insulating joints		11.52
25 - 3/4" Conduit Covers	@ .055	1.38
25 - 1/2" Conduit Covers	@ .04	1.00
25 - 1" Conduits	@ .50	12.50
35 - 3/4" Conduits	@ .30	10.50
40 - Pull chain sockets	@ .06	24.00*
20 - Fuse Plugs	@ .60	12.00
30 - Switch Plates		3.89
6 - Base plug receptacles	@ .70	4.20
10 - Push switches	@ .45	4.50
60 - Switch boxes	@ .22	12.20*
100 - 1/2" Bushings	@ .03	3.00
10 - Combined switch and cut-outs	@ .80	8.00
100 - 1/2" Lock Nuts		1.25
12 - 1/2" Greenfield connectors	@ .05	.60
4 lbs. insulating tape		.70
1 lb Rubber tape		.21
75 - Tungsten Lamps	@ .20	15.00
25 Shade Holders	@ .07	1.75
50 - 1/2" Outlet boxes	@ .10	5.00
6 Lighting arresters	@ .50	3.00
1500 Ft. - No. 14 Duplex copper wire		45.54
100 Ft. Greenfield Conduit		6.50
500 Ft. - No. 14 R.C. Copper wire		11.95
500 Ft. - No. 14 R.C. Weather proof		11.95
200 Ft. - 1" conduit	@ .12	24.00
500 Ft - 3/4" conduit	@ .10	50.00
500 Ft.- 1/2" conduit		26.35
35 Gal. ready mixed paint	@ 2.00	70.00
25 Gal. Varnish	@ 3.00	75.00
6 Gal. paint remover		11.25
10 Cans color in oil	@ .40	4.00
2 Gal. Shellac	@ 3.50	7.00
1 Gal. Seam Filler		3.20
1 Tub Putty		3.50
150 Ft. - 2" Black pipe	@ .09	13.50
150 Ft. - 1 & 1/2" Black Pipe	@ .08	12.00
150 Ft. - 1 & 3/4" Black Pipe	@ .07	10.50
300 Ft. - 1" Gal. Water pipe	@ .09	27.00
200 Ft. - 3/4" Gal. Water pipe	@ .06	12.00
200 Ft. - 1/2" Gal. Water pipe	@ .05	10.00
300 lbs. Galv. Pipe fittings	@ .15	45.00
1 Hot Water Boiler 40 gal.		12.00
1 Laundry Stove		+31.00
TOTAL APPRAISAL FOR ELECTRICAL SUPPLIES -		**671.44**

MACHINERY AND TOOLS AT THE *BOLDT YACHT HOUSE* IN 1917

shipyard boiler & engine in good repair		150.00
spile driver	1 year's use	150.00
hammer, old	1000 lbs. weight	50.00
engine, old but usable		100.00
steam hoist, in poor repair		75.00
concrete mixer, needs lot of repair		50.00
3 steam drills in poor condition @ $25.00 each		75.00
1 derrick, in fair repair		50.00
	total	**$700.00**

ICING MACHINERY

2 Ice Plows	@ $15.00 each	30.00
10 pairs Tongs	@ $1.00 each	10.00
Slides		40.00
Spudding Irons and grab hooks		20.00
new Rumsey Pump (Water)		800.00
1 old pump (Gould) 15 years old		150.00
1 old pump (Gould) 6 years old		150.00
1 engine & dynamo (Otto Engine) 15 years old		700.00
1 Sebastian Lathe 14" centers		250.00
1 old second-hand lathe (fair condition)		50.00
1 drill press (fair condition)		200.00
1 milling machine second-hand		120.00
1 grinder		40.00
miscellaneous machine shop tools		200.00
1 sand pump 6" old & second-hand		75.00
1 sand pump 10" old & second-hand		200.00

TOTAL APPRAISAL FOR ICING MACHINERY - 3,035.00

TOTAL APPRAISAL MACHINERY AND TOOLS   700.00

TOTAL APPRAISAL FOR ELECTRICAL SUPPLIES - + 671.44

GRAND TOTAL $4,406.44

In March, 1917, *George C. Boldt Jr.*, and his sister, *Mrs. Alfred Graham Miles*, tendered to the *United States Government*, rent free, the *Boldt Yacht House* with its construction plant attached. It is said to have been the largest and most completely equipped private building of its kind in the country. The *United States* was involved in *World War I* at the time of the offer by the *Boldt* family.

The payroll for the staff at the *Boldt Yacht House* in 1918 was $1,090.00. The summary of general cash receipts from January 1, 1918 to December 31, 1918 were as follows:

scow **Mary** -	400.00	Leopold & Co – stone – 181.50	
scow **Helen** -	350.00	motor oil – 78.74	
motor boat **Algeria** -	100.00	gasoline - 260.74	
old boat **Cricket** –	15.00	part of old windlass – 7.50	
old Jencick engine	50.00	**Total $528.78**	
storage of **Curlew** –	100.00		
storage of launches –	100.00		
docking **Presque Isle** –	50.00		
hire of scows –	751.50		
hire of **Squab** –	+218.50		
Total $2,135.00			

Another interesting thing also happened in 1918 when *George C. Boldt Jr.* and his sister *Louise Clover Boldt Miles* opened *Boldt Castle* on *Heart Island* to the general public. Work on this new summer home for the *Boldt* family was begun in 1900 and ceased when their mother *Louise Augusta Kehrer Boldt* died on January 7, 1904. Visitors were now allowed to enjoy roaming the estate and wonder with curiosity what it would have been like had it been completed.

The Boldt Yacht House and much of the *George C. Boldt* fleet of boats, was sold to *Mr. Edward J. Noble* in 1922, along with *Boldt Castle* on *Heart Island*, and the entire farm operation *Mr. Boldt* built on Wellesley Island. Under *Edward John Noble's* ownership the use of the *Boldt Yacht House* was used pretty much the same as in the past with boat storage and repairs. The building itself however saw little to no upkeep or improvements over the years.

EDWARD JOHN NOBLE

Mr. Edward John Noble was a northern New York man who was born in Gouverneur, New York, the son of *Mr.* and *Mrs. H. H. Noble*. He was a *Yale* graduate who went to New York City and organized the *Mint Products Company.* This company manufactured the *Life Saver*, the celebrated candy with the hole in it. Through an extensive advertising campaign the *Life Savers* are known in every section of the world. During *World War I* he left his business to serve throughout the war as a major in the ordinance department. He owned a beautiful summer home opposite Alexandria Bay, on the Canadian side of the river near Rockport, Ontario, and called it *"Journey's End."* It is located at *Echo Point* on the Canadian channel and is one of the finest in that section. *Mr. Noble* had always been passionately fond of the St. Lawrence River.

It is obvious that *Mr. Noble* would use the *Boldt Yacht House* for his watercraft. Although he sold off some of the *George C. Boldt* fleet, *Mr. Noble* never attained such a vast assortment of boats. Certainly he would use the *Boldt Yacht House* because of its' proximity to the social center of the Thousand Island region which was the *Thousand Island Yacht Club*, of which he was a member, and the *Thousand Island Club*, which he now owned. The *Boldt Yacht House* would eventually be referred to as the *Noble Yacht House*. One of *Mr. Noble's* boats was the *Snail,* which you can see and read about on page 84.

BELOW IS THOUGHT TO BE *MR. FREDERICK W. ADAMS* AT HIS BOAT WORKS IN ALEXANDRIA BAY. THE ST. LAWRENCE RIVER WAS VERY HIGH IN MAY 1929. *MR. ADAMS* WAS EMPLOYED BY *BOLDT* AS SUPERVISOR OF HIS FLEET AND BUILDER OF BOATS

It was during May of 1929 that high water caused damage running into thousands of dollars along the St. Lawrence River. *The Boldt Yacht House* suffered little damage according to *Mr. Edward J. Noble* owner of the property. He stated *"We are protected from the southwesterly winds which caused most of the damage in this region, and for that reason my property has escaped damage in many instances when others are less fortunate. If we should get a strong wind from another direction, it would probably be a different story."* Mr. Noble went on to say *"The rise in the river this year is quite inexplicable and river men here seem to have no reason to offer. It is generally predicted that the water will begin to go down about the middle of June."* About the only inconvenience was the necessity of building upper decks on most of the docks to permit the landing of boats.

Mr. Harold Comstock, was superintendent of the former *George C. Boldt* property, and now the *Edward John Noble* estate in 1935. He and his wife *Pearl* and their three children, *Arlene*, *Beverly* and brother *Harold Jr.* lived in the *Boldt Yacht House* from 1935 until 1944. Young *Beverly* was 8 years old in 1935 and would recall the hardships of island living. *"Winter travel was more hazardous and difficult in the early years. "One crossed over the ice pushing an ice punt or walking, jabbing a pike hole in the ice in front of you."*

ABOVE IS THE *BOLDT YACHT HOUSE* IN WINTER WITH WHAT IS THOUGHT TO BE SOME OF THE *HAROLD COMSTOCK* FAMILY. THEY LIVED AT THE *BOLDT YACHT HOUSE* FROM 1935 TO 1944

Beverly Comstock also remembered the good times, *"biking on the islands many roads, roller skating on its sidewalks, roaming in the woods, swimming off the main dock, exploring the canals, and surrounding area in our row boats or my brother's outboard, watching all sorts of lake and passenger cruise boats going up and down the river, playing golf in the off season."*

When *Harold Comstock and his family* moved from the *Boldt Yacht House* in 1944, *Mr. James McAloon* became caretaker of the property for *Edward John Noble*. He came from Connecticut to Alexandria Bay, New York with his family. His son *George* entered the *United States Army* during *World War II* shortly after arriving, but spent many summers working at the yacht house during his collage years. He especially remembered polishing the large wooden boats that were kept there. Young *George McAloon* would eventually become an attorney.

Over a period of time the *Boldt Yacht House* became the victim of neglect and the elements. The structure slipped into a state of disrepair. Most of the *Boldt* fleet had been sold off and the building found little use. The houseboat *LaDuchesse* was moored inside there until 1943 when it was sold to *Mr. Andrew McNally III*. *Mr. Edward John Noble*, who owned the yacht house, died in 1958. Wisely he formed his namesake foundation in 1940. In time *The Edward John Noble Foundation*, obtained stasis for the *Boldt Yacht House* to be on the *National Register of Historical Places*.

In 1976 the *Boldt Yacht House* was nominated for consideration to *The National Register of Historical Places*. Owner of the yacht house was the *Edward John Noble Foundation* of 32 East 57th Street in New York City. *Mr. Raymond W. Smith*, a *Historic Preservation Program Assistant* with the *New York State Parks and Recreation* prepared the application, which was dated July 1977. *The Boldt Yacht House* had been evaluated according to the criteria and procedures set forth by *The National Park Service*, and was included in the *National Register* on October 25, 1977.

It was in the fall of 1976 that the *Edward John Noble Foundation* offered the *Boldt Yacht House*, *Boldt Castle*, the *Thousand Islands Club*, and more of the *Boldt/Noble* property to the *Thousand Islands Bridge Authority* of Alexandria Bay, New York. *Mr. Donald C. Andrus*, clerk of the *Jefferson County Board of Supervisors* stressed that the properties would be gifts to the *Thousand Islands Bridge Authority* and would not cost the bridge users or county taxpayers any funds. The properties needed renovation, and a special task force looked into the proposal.

The task force was called the *Thousand Islands Bridge Authority Properties Development Committee* and included *Alfred Tauroney*, *Vincent Dee*, and *Ken Howard* from the *Thousand Islands Bridge Authority*. Other members were county chairman *Robert Austin* and his administrative assistant *Donald Andrus* from the *Jefferson County Board of Supervisors*. They met in January of 1978 to develop plans for the properties.

By 1978 the *Edward John Noble Foundation* gave the *Boldt Yacht House* and all the former *Boldt* property to the *Thousand Islands Bridge Authority*. During that summer *State Parks and Recreation Commissioner Orin Lehman* announced that the *Boldt Yacht House* had been listed on the *National Register of Historical Places*. *Commissioner Lehman* served as the *State Historic Preservation Officer* and was responsible for New York State's efforts on behalf of the federal program to recognize and preserve historic resources. He said: *"The continuous use of the yacht house as a marine service facility and its significance is an important visual and historical reminder of the American "Age of Opulence."*

In addition to recognition of historical and architectural values, and eligibility for federal funding, *National Register* listing gives the *Boldt Yacht House* a measure of protection. A project that might have a negative impact on the site must be carefully reviewed and justified before it can be funded or licensed by a federal agency.

With a $100,000.00 grant from the *Edward John Noble foundation*, the *Thousand Islands Bridge Authority* quickly instituted a rehabilitation project that would stave off additional deterioration and embarked on a well-planned stabilization/restoration project of the *Boldt Yacht House* to repair the structure to its original state.

The *Thousand Islands Bridge Authority* put the *Boldt Yacht House* property into the hands of a very fine and capable engineer, *Mr. Dale Fikes*. As *Special Projects Supervisor* for the *Thousand Island Bridge Authority, Mr. Fikes* began the long and challenging duty of renovating the *Boldt Yacht House* property. Decay, aging, neglect and vandalism had scared both the interior and exterior. Assessing the entire complex, *Mr. Fikes* and his crew began the initial job of clearing and cleaning up the place.

One of the first phases of the work was to build new cribs and dock. Then attention was turned to the window and roof repairs. The original wood shingled roofs have been replaced with modern asphalt shingle covering, though the original inner wood sheathing remains intact. *Mr. Alfred M. Tauroney*, secretary/treasurer of the *Thousand Islands Bridge Authority* and chairman of the *Thousand Islands Bridge Authority Properties Development Committee* oversaw the direction of the work.

The work at restoring both the *Boldt Yacht House* and *Boldt Castle* on *Heart Island* by the *Thousand Islands Bridge Authority* has been, and is, a very costly and time-consuming undertaking. Funds to cover the cost came from other former *Boldt* property given to them by the *Edward John Noble Foundation,* which they in turn sold off. In addition, grant money, public contributions, and admission fees from *Boldt Castle* visitor's go to this massive undertaking.

The *Thousand Islands Bridge Authority* commissioned the architectural firm of *Stephen W. Yaussi* and *Robert S. Aceti* of 220 Sterling Street, Watertown, New York, in the spring of 1984 to research the *Boldt* property. The primary importance was further stabilization and repairs as necessary. With the *Thousand Islands Bridge Authority* limited in their funding, they were submitting grant applications via both the public and private route in order to continue the reconstruction and repair project.

Law Brothers Contracting Corporation of Lyons Falls and Watertown, New York were hired to work on the *Boldt Yacht House.* This firm was founded in 1898 and had a wide area of expertise and skills. To illustrate this point, *Mr. Blair Law*, president of the firm that bears his name, cited the renovation project his firm was doing at *the Boldt Yacht House.* To safely and expeditiously renovate the structure's interior, the firm had decided to use one of its most basic rigging techniques, sky climbers. *"This system operates by electric motor. It is easy to erect and very effective"* said *Mr. Law. "Without this rigging, it would take us twice the time and would incur tremendous risk to not only the structure's integrity, but our people's safety as well."*

Bids for contracting some of the restoration of the *Boldt Yacht House* were made. Awarded for the façade work was the contracting firm of *PLC Construction* of Alexandria Bay, NY. The building received new shake shingles siding, new trim, fresh paint, and restoration of the huge bay doors. The original *Boldt* crest was replaced with one made of clear all heart Redwood and weighs 300 pounds. This wooden work of art was designed and handcrafted by *Barney Sign Company* of Johnstown, NY. It took two and one half months to complete the crest. The artwork carries the theme of the heart and scrolls that are an integral part of the *Boldt* family.

The sides of the yacht house restoration was done by *Thousand Islands Bridge Authority* employees. Two of those employees were *Dick Dack* and *Dale Leeson.* The long-term goal was to eventually open the yacht house to the public. Work toward this end required provision for restrooms, parking, and the establishment of a boat shuttle system for transportation of visitors. The restroom work was done by *Palco Ltd.* of Lyons Falls, New York. The work at the yacht house was done to make it handicap accessible. The installation of smoke and fire alarms as well as a sprinkler system was installed.

Finally after many years of hard work and the outlay of $900,000.00 since 1977, the *Boldt Yacht House* was opened to the general public for the first time on Friday, June 21, 1996. It must have been a very proud time for *Mr. Dale Fikes*, the *Thousand Islands Bridge Authority's Special Projects Supervisor* who oversaw the renovation work. An opening ceremony was held to mark the occasion. The grand opening ceremony was attended by community leaders of Jefferson County and local government officials as well as *State Assemblyman H. Robert Nortz*, Republican from Cape Vincent, New York and *State Senator James W. Wright*, Republican from Watertown, New York. *Russell Wilcox, Executive Director* for the *Thousand Islands Bridge Authority*, briefly recounted the history of the authority's restoration project on the yacht house since they acquired it in 1977.

The Antique Boat Museum of Clayton, New York has loaned the *Thousand Islands Bridge Authority* seven boats for display, including three that were once owned by *George C. Boldt.* They are the *P.D.Q, (Pretty Dam Quick), This* and *That. Antique Boat Museum* executive director *Mr. William G. Danforth* told a little about each of the craft on display and acknowledged their donors, some of whom were present.

Mr. Danford also commented on the cooperation between the *Antique Boat Museum* and the *Thousand Islands Bridge Authority. "At one time when politicians in Washington have redefined gridlock, we in the North Country are showing that partnership between public agencies, government and private institutions are possible and that together we can create an economic synergy that will revitalize the area."*

In attendance were hundreds of interested visitors. Among them was this author and *Mr. Andrew McNally III*, owner of the houseboat *LaDuchesse* that *George C.* Boldt once owned. He remarked to me that no mention of *George C. Boldt* was made. Sadly we both remarked at how unfortunate this was. Also in attendance was *Beverly Comstock Keeler* of Jacksonville, Florida, and Attorney *George McAloon* of Alexandria Bay, New York, both of whom had lived in the yacht house at one time and offered their reminiscences.

Mrs. Keeler lived on the premises when her father, *Harold Comstock*, was superintendent of the estate. Her mother *Pearl*, sister *Arlene*, and brother *Harold Jr.* lived there also. *Mrs. Keeler* moved there in 1935 when she was 8 years old, and left in 1944, and had not returned until Friday, June 21, 1996. *Mrs. Keeler* recalled the hardships of island living before the *Thousand Islands Bridge* opened in 1938. Also speaking at the opening ceremony was *Mr. Donald Grant*, chairman of the *Thousand Islands Bridge Authority* and *Mr. Shane Sanford*, property manager for *Boldt Castle*.

Part of the festivities at the *Boldt Yacht House* on June 21, 1996 was a special postal cancellation stating *"Boldt Yacht House Station, Alexandria Bay, New York 13607,"* by the *United States Postal Service*.

Displayed in the *Boldt Yacht House* is antique watercraft and various turn-of-the-century displays with a nautical theme. Visitors can now view the actual utilitarian function of this unique building. Many historic photographs are displayed complementing the entire exhibition. A large display of antique outboard motors, rowing and racing skiffs and other items relating to boating are there also. There is a portion of the Captain's quarters' open for viewing. Oak ceiling, moldings, wainscoting, ornately carved balusters and newel posts, characterize the circular tower. The fireplaces are of cut and fitted stone.

For access to the *Boldt Yacht House* there is a free shuttle service from *Boldt Castle*. The *Thousand Islands Bridge Authority* purchased a 45-foot long pontoon boat that has a 14-foot beam. The 49-passenger shuttle was obtained from *Susuehanna Santee Boat Works* of Lancaster, Pennsylvania. It is powered by twin 115 hp. Mariner outboards, and was built at a cost of $65,000.00. Vehicular access to the yacht house is by appointment only with the *Thousand Islands Bridge Authority*.

And so the visitors came. That is all 14,669 visitors the first year and bringing in $27,729.00 in admission fees. Ongoing restoration of the yacht house continues as well as maintenance needs. Marketing the yacht house and *Boldt Castle* on *Heart Island* to the tourist is also an ongoing effort by the *Thousand Islands Bridge Authority* and the *1000 Islands International Council* at Alexandria Bay, New York.

The present day *Boldt Yacht House* attraction provides an incalculable economic value to the tourism industry in the Thousand Island Region, benefiting both the *United States* and *Canadian* interest. The *Thousand Islands Bridge Authority* will continue to preserve the *Boldt Yacht House* property for the present and future generations to enjoy. It is opened from mid-May to mid-October with a very low entrance fee. ($2.00 per adult - $1.00 per child – age 6-12). The yacht house is opened from 10:00 am to 6:00 pm daily. You may write them at *Thousand Islands Bridge Authority* – Collins Landing - P.O. Box 428 - Alexandria Bay, New York 13607. Email – info@boldtcastle.com or at their web site. www.boldtcastle.com or call them at 1-800-847-5263.

BOLDT'S BOATS
For communications between various properties at the Thousand Island estate of *George C. Boldt*, as well as for the staff, a fleet of vessels was available. Being in the midst of the *"Venice of America"* it was fitting that nothing should be lacking in the way of boats. This is an account of over 70 watercraft once owned by the *Boldt* family. The watercraft is listed alphabetically.

SUMMARY VALUE OF *GEORGE C. BOLDT'S* BOATS AT THE TIME OF HIS DEATH, DECEMBER 5, 1916

1. **ARK** - 50 foot scow	- 22 foot beam	- 51 tons	- built 1900	250.00
2. **CLOVER** - 81 foot steam yacht	- 10 foot 9 in. beam	- 27 tons	- built 1901	4,000.00
3. **COCOA** - sailing yacht				
4. **COUNTRY CLUB** - 30 foot motor boat	- 7 foot beam		- built 1905	200.00
5. **CRESCENT** - 50 foot steam yacht	- 9 foot 6 inch beam		- built 1895	2,000.00
6. **CRICKET** - 24 foot motor boat	- 9 foot beam			
7. **DAIRY MAID** - 20 foot motor boat	- 4 foot beam		- built 1900	25.00
8. **DERRICK #1** - 40 foot flat scow	- 16 foot beam	- 23 tons	- built 1900	150.00
9. **DERRICK #2** - 25 foot flat scow	- 12 foot beam		- built 1896	50.00
10. **DIXIE** - 19 foot motor boat	- 4 foot 6 inch beam		- built 1903	25.00
11. **DREDGE** - 70 foot dredge	- 29 foot beam		- built 1897	1,200.00
12. **ELLEN** - 65 foot flat scow	- 18 foot beam	- 73 tons	- built 1898	250.00
13. **ETHEL DALE** - 30 foot motor boat	- 6 foot beam		- built 1915	1,800.00
14. **FROST KING** - 30 foot motor boat	- 6 foot 6 inch beam			
15. **FROST KING II** - 32 foot motor boat	- 6 foot 6 inch beam		- built 1909	300.00
16. **GOLF** - 22 foot motor boat	- 4 foot 6 inch beam			
17. **HEART** - naphtha launch			(1898)	
18. **LADUCHESSE** - 104 foot houseboat	- 21 foot beam	- 247 tons	- built 1903	12,000.00
19. **LOUISE** - 102 foot steam yacht	- 14 foot beam	- 49 tons	- built 1893	5,000.00
20. **MARY** - 65 foot flat scow	- 16 foot beam	- 73 tons	- built 1898	250.00
21. **P.D.Q.** - 39 foot motor boat	- 4 foot 6 inch beam		- built 1904	
22. **PRESTO** - 80 feet 4 in. steam yacht	- 9 foot 7 inch beam	- 22 tons	- built 1897	
23. **QUEEN** - 50 foot 7 inch steam tug	- 14 foot beam	- 29 tons	- built 1897	
24. **SCOUT** - 36 foot motor boat	- 6 foot 4 inch beam		- built 1912	1,000.00
25. **SENIOR** - 45 foot motor boat	- 8 foot 6 inch beam		- built 1912	3,600.00
26. **SNOW QUEEN** - 20 foot motor boat	- 5 foot beam			
27. **SQUAB** - 38 foot fire boat	- 10 foot beam		- built 1914	1,500.00
28. **THAT** - 28 foot motor boat	- 5 foot beam		- built 1910	
29. **THIS** - 28 foot motor boat	- 5 foot beam		- built 1910	
30. **TIA JUANA** - 30 foot motor boat	- 5 foot beam			
31. **TOZER** - 22 foot motor boat	- 5 foot beam			
32. **TROUBLER**				
33. **TURTLE** - 40 foot flat scow	- 18 foot beam	- 45 ton	- built 1906	200.00
19 skiffs	- 18 foot		- built 1907	570.00
2 dump scows	- 50 foot - 12 beam - 125 cubic yards		- built 1898	400.00
7 row boats			- built 1912	150.00
1 canoe			- built 1905	20.00
62 watercraft			**GRAND TOTAL VALUE**	**$34,940.00**

Mr. Francis S. Hutchins, personal attorney for *George C. Boldt*, of the law firm of *Baldwin & Hutchins*, 27 Pine Street, New York City, filed an affidavit of appraisal of boats, with the Surrogate's Court, New York County, in the matter of appraisal under the transfer tax law of the estate of *Mr. Boldt. Mr. James H. Hutchinson* of Alexandria Bay, New York, did the appraisal and reads as follows:

"James H. Hutchinson, being duly sworn, deposes and says: I reside at Alexandria Bay, Jefferson County, State of New York. I am a member of the firm of Hutchinson Brothers Boat Builders, doing business at Alexandria Bay, Jefferson County, State of New York.

'I have been actively and constantly engaged as a boat builder for more than 15 years, during which time I have personally taken part in the construction and superintendence of boats, also have bought and sold boats, similar to those as more fully described and set forth in the annexed schedule, and by reason of such experience, I am thoroughly familiar with the values of boats, as described herein.

'That during the month of June, 1917, I personally examined and inspected for the purpose of appraising the boats said to have belonged to the decedent herein, at the time of his demise, December 5, 1916, and have appraised as of that date the boats and appurtenances thereto as set forth in the inventory hereto attached, and this deponent is of the opinion that if the boats, dredges, scows, etc., as per annexed schedule, had been offered for sale on the day of death of this decedent, they would not have realized more than $35,040.00, which was the clear market value thereof on the said 5th day of December, 1916." This affidavit was signed by *Mr. James H. Hutchinson* and *Mr. Charles Putnam* was the *Notary Public* that this was sworn before on July 14, 1917 in Jefferson County, New York.

The - * (asterisk) - refers to the boats, dredges, scows, etc., that *Mr. James H. Hutchinson* appraised on July 14, 1917. The vessels were housed at the *Boldt Yacht House* on Fern Island off Wellesley Island, Alexandria Bay, New York.

ARK -* - Listed as part of the working fleet, the *Ark* was 50 feet with a 22 foot beam. Its' tonnage was 51 tons and was believed to be built in 1900. Please bare in mind as you read about Mr. Boldt's *"working fleet"* that these vessels were used in the construction of *Boldt Castle,* the yacht house, and his large farm operation on Welesley Island.

In May of 1904 a morning fire at Thousand Island Park, causing an estimated damage of $20,000.00 destroyed 9 cottages. The fire broke out about 10:00 am and assistance was summoned from Clayton, Alexandria Bay, and other communities. At 1 pm the fire was under control. The cottages destroyed were at the rear of the *Colombian Hotel.* None of their contents were saved, and no one was reported to have been injured. A man who was raking up leaves and cleaning lawns set fire to a pile of leaves, and soon the fire spread trough the dry grass and beneath the cottage of *Dr. Bailey* who was from Adams Center, New York. The fire then spread to the adjoining cottages.

In response to a call for help, the Alexandria Bay engine and hose carts were quickly loaded on board the scow *Ark* and in tow of the tug *Queen* started up river, accompanied by about 30 firemen. The *Queen* was also owned by *George C. Boldt* and will be described under its own name.

Listed with the inventory of boats, scows, dredges, etc. belonging to the estate of *George Charles Boldt Sr.,* deceased, contained in the *Boldt Yacht House* at the Thousand Islands, Alexandria Bay, New York, Jefferson County, and done by *Mr. James H. Hutchinson* on July 14, 1917, was a flat scow named *Ark.* By 1917 it was badly in need of repair and appraised at $250.00 at that time. *Mr. Charles Putnam* was the Notary Public who signed the affidavit of appraisal.

CALYPSO   In the summer of 1898 *George C. Boldt* hired a handsome steam yacht, the *Calypso*, and placed it at the disposal of the guests of the *Waldorf-Astoria* hotels that he managed in New York City, to take his patrons out upon the waters of the Sound, and in the harbor or the Hudson River. For this deluxe service he charged ten dollars a seat, and included luncheon aboard the craft. The *Calypso*, which carried but twenty-five passengers, could be chartered for $150.00 for the entire day.

To get his guests to the *Calypso* and back again Mr. *Boldt* set up a four-in-hand coaching service - it was, of course, long before the day of the motorcar - and this feature of the day's outing proving so popular in itself, it was extended, with the aid of *Mr. T. Suffern Tailer*, to Woodmansten, and later to Arrowhead in New York City.

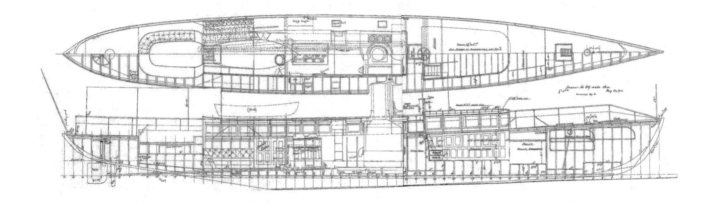

1901 DRAWINGS OF THE 80 FOOT STEAM YACHT *DAWN* WHICH *GEORGE C. BOLDT* RENAMED THE *CLOVER*

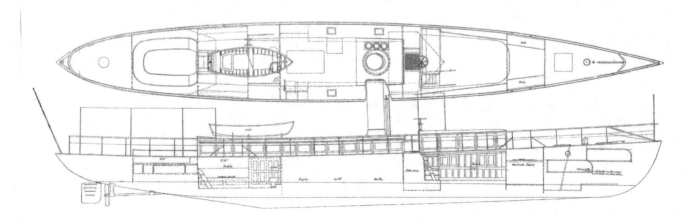

THE STEAM YACHT *CLOVER* WAS A PICTURESQUE FAST YACHT, DESIGNED AND CONSTRUCTED IN THE *HERRESHOFF* TRADITION. BELOW THE *CLOVER* IS TO THE LEFT, WHILE THE MOTOR BOAT *LITTLE JEFF* IS ON THE RIGHT. *GEORGE C. BOLDT* DID NOT OWN THE *LITTLE JEFF*.

CLOVER - * - The *Clover* was originally known as the *Dawn* and was designed by *Mr. Nathaniel G. Herreshoff* and was built by the *Herreshoff Manufacturing Company* at Bristol, Rhode Island in July 1901. Hull number was 212; construction was of wood. Her specifications were as follows: net tons, 18; gross tons, 27; overall length, 81 feet. At the waterline she was 72 feet. She had a 10 foot 6 inch beam. Depth was 3 feet 4 inches. Draft was 3 feet 6 inches. Her original power plant was a *Herreshoff Triple Expansion Steam Engine*, 6 and 1/4, 10 inch by 16 inch and 9 inches of stroke. Boiler was bent tube and the screw was 36 inches. A *Seabury Water Tube Boiler* was installed in 1910. The yacht's registration number was 157623.

THE STEAM YACHT *CLOVER* IN FRONT OF *GEORGE C. BOLDT'S SWISS CHALET* RENTAL PROPERTY

Below deck was the forecastle with 3 berths, 2 were on the port side, and 1 on the starboard side. Behind that was a wardrobe closet with shelves above on either side. A stairway led to the hatch above on the deck. Behind this was the forward cabin, which measured 11 feet 8 inches and had a stairway that led to the deck. Behind this cabin was a storeroom. A hatch below the pilot station gave access to this area. The hatch measured 20 inches square.

To the rear of the storage area was the boiler and then the engine room, which measured 16 feet 4 inches. A ladder provided access to this room with a hatch on the deck. This room had a workbench. A 13-inch by 9-foot copper water tank below the boiler held 254 gallons of water. The *Clover* had a simplex vertical featherweight air pump, which was manufactured by the *George F. Blake Company*. The anchor davit would be used for a 57-pound anchor.

The quadrant for the engine room telegraph was cast bronze with a file finish. Brass stanchions where used and had a 3/4-inch diameter steel bar put inside the brass pipe for 9 and 1/2 inches. The stanchions were 28 and 5/8 inches high. The deck housetop was made of 1/2 inch pine and had a canvas covering. 3/16-inch plate glass was used in the windows. Hatches were 21 inches by 20 inches and were made of mahogany. The rudder or steering quadrant drawings were dated November 5, 1900.

The aft cabin measured 6 feet 10 inches and had settee berths. Forward from the aft cabin was a bathroom with toilet, wash basin and closets. A stairway led to the aft deck, which measured 8 feet 6 inches. Above the aft cabin was the 11 feet 6 inch lifeboat. The flagpole on the aft deck was 9 feet 6 inches long. The rudder or steering quadrant drawings were also dated November 5, 1900. There was a settee on the port side of the pilot's station and a hatch with stairway leading to the forward cabin on the starboard side. This hatch measured 2 feet 10 and 1/2 inches long. Woodwork throughout the *Clover* was *Spanish Cedar*.

This launch type steam yacht *Clover* had a full deckhouse, raised long trunk cabin and cockpit, and her accommodations for cruising were extensive. There was no aft cockpit; the flush deck extended to the stern. The awning, full width, extended from the smokestack to the stern, covering the trunk cabin as well as the aft deck. The awning served a dual purpose. It provided shade from the sun, protection from the rain, and kept the deck and passengers protected from the smoke and soot from the smokestack. The drawings for the awning were dated February 4th and 12th 1901.

The *Clover* did not seem to acquire the notoriety of her contemporaries that the *Herreshoff Manufacturing Company* built in the same year of 1901, the *Jean, Lotus Seeker, Stroller* and the *Now Then,* yet she must have attained their average speed of 20 mph and was listed as having 250 horsepower.

The Herreshoff Manufacturing Company that built the *Clover* was founded by *John Brown Herreshoff* in 1863. In 1878 he took into partnership his younger brother *Nathanael Greene Herreshoff* who attended the *Massachusetts Institute of Technology*. Nat was employed by the famed *Corliss Engine Works* in Providence for nine years. Upon joining his brother's firm of boat builders, he concentrated initially on designing steam vessels. In the early 1890's, he turned his attention to designing sailing yachts. As a trained engineer, *Captain Nathanael Herreshoff* possessed a craftsman's touch for tools and materials.

The Herreshoff Manufacturing plant included complete facilities for turning out fully equipped vessels. It did not rely on other suppliers to guarantee delivery of parts, or to match its standard of quality. Equipped with its own foundry, sawmill, and sail loft, as well as sheds and machine shops, the plant's resources permitted *Herreshoff* to design and manufacture boats as systems. That is, every element was engineered to ensure each vessel would function optimally. Today there stands the *Herreshoff Marine Museum* at 7 Burnside Street in Bristol, Rhode Island that displays much of this company's rich tradition. Call them at (401)253-5000 or fax (401)253-6222 or check out the web site at www.herrshoff.org.

The port of registry for the *Clover* was New York City in 1910, the same year Mr. Boldt obtained the *Dawn* and renamed it the *Clover*. Its former owner was *Mr. J. S. Newberry* of Detroit, Michigan. It is thought, and somewhat obvious that *Mr. Boldt* obtained this vessel for his only daughter *Louise Clover* and named the boat in her honor. *Louise Clover* was 27 years old when her father purchased the *Dawn*. She was married for 3 years to *Alfred Graham Miles* and together they had a daughter also named *Clover* who was born to them in 1910. In her later years this child became *Mrs. Clover Boldt Baird* of *Hopewell Hall*. Like all the other watercraft in the *Boldt* fleet the *Clover* would be used for the pleasure of the family and their friends.

George C. Boldt was a member of the *Chippewa Yacht Club* at Chippewa Bay, New York in the Thousand Islands and the *Clover* was listed in their 1912 directory.

By 1913 the port of registry for the *Clover* was Cape Vincent, New York and Alexandria Bay, New York and was the homeport. The *Clover* was listed on the inventory of boats appraised on July 14, 1917 that belonged to *Mr. Boldt*. It was valued at $4,000.00 at that time. In 1918 the *Clover* was listed in *Town and Country Magazine* for rent along with other former *George C. Boldt* boats and properties. The *Clover* was listed as belonging to the estate of *Mr. Boldt* until 1920.

In 1922, the *Clover* was owned by *The Prudy Boat Company* of Trenton, Michigan and was her homeport. It is believed that the steam power plant was removed in 1922 for a 1924 account listed the *Clover* as having a *Speedway Gasoline Engine* installed, 4 stroke, 8 cylinder, 5 and 3/4 inch of bore and 7 inch stroke. Although it was powerful, it is doubted that it could have produced as much speed as the steam engine.

A. C. Webb of Montauk, New York had purchased the *Clover* in 1929. Her homeport became Miami, Florida. From 1938 to 1948, *Mr. Julius R. Sahr* was the owner. New York, New York was the homeport during that time. Another picture of *Clover* can be seen on page 45.

COCOA – was a sailing yacht. A July 24, 1896 article tells about *George C. Boldt's* sailing yacht *Cricket*, which got the best of *James H. Oliphant's Florence* and *Hayden's* yacht in a series of races at Alexandria Bay. It is believed that the writer of that article got the name wrong, as the *Cricket* was a motor boat and the *Cocoa* was a sailing yacht *Mr. Boldt* owned. A May 1898 article states that *George C. Boldt* was building a new 20-foot sailing yacht.

AN EARLY VIEW OF *HEART ISLAND* SHOWING THE WOOD FRAMED *HART COTTAGE* THAT WAS REMOVED IN 1900. THE SAIL BOAT AT THE BOAT HOUSE MAY HAVE BEEN THE *COCOA*

COUNTRY CLUB - * - was built around 1905 and was 30 feet long and had a 7 foot beam. This motor boat was propelled by gasoline. The hull construction was of wood and appraised for $200.00 on July 14, 1917.

BELOW A *CERTIFICATE OF INSPECTION* FOR STEAM PLEASURE YACHTS WAS ISSUED TO THE *CRECENT* ON JUNE 20, 1910 AND WAS DONE BY *ROBERT CHESTNUT*. THE CERTIFICATE EXPIRED ON JUNE 15, 1911.

SHOWN FROM ST. ELMO ISLAND THE *CRESCENT* HEADING UP RIVER. THE ESTATE CALLED *HOPEWELL HALL* IS AT THE LEFT AND WAS OWNED BY MR. BOLDT. *CASTLE REST* IS THE ESTATE IN THE CENTER WITH *NOBBY ISLAND* TO THE RIGHT.

CRESCENT - * - It was in early summer of 1895 that the new steamer *Crescent* was built for the *Thousand Island Transit Company* who had *Mr. William Charles Browning* as one of its' directors. The company had been incorporated for the transportation of passengers and baggage, and to facilitate communications between and among cottages at the Thousand Islands and nearby villages. The company used several steam yachts for this purpose. One of these was the *Crescent*, which was built in 1895. Other directors of *The Thousand Island Transit Company* were *James H. Oliphant, Edward W. Dewey, Henry R. Heath, Daniel C. McEwen, William McAlfee, Henry A. Lloughlin, J. W. Jackson* and *William Townsend*.

The *Crescent* was built at a length of 50 feet and had a 9 foot 6-inch beam. Her hull construction was of wood. She was built as a steam yacht and later converted to a gas engine, which was a 60 or 75 hp. *Sterling* engine. With this power plant she could glide through the water at a rate of 13 miles per hour.

In July of 1895 *Captain Bottom* was at the wheel when the *Crescent* made a trial trip with a pleasant party of the directors and families were on board. The little vessel made excellent time and refreshments were served. Everyone had a good time and the boat was going to be a great convenience to the islanders.

THE STEAM BOAT *CRESCENT* AT ALEXANDRIA BAY, NEW YORK. *ALSTER TOWER* ON
HEART ISLAND CAN BE SEEN IN THE BACKGROUND TO THE RIGHT

During the summer of 1896 the *Crescent* made six round trips every day between Alexandria Bay and Central Park in the Thousand Islands.

A newspaper article dating 1898 listed a forty-seven foot steam yacht named *Crescent* built in 1898, and that a *Mr. Livingston* would be the pilot for the season.

The *Crescent* was used as the *Thousand Islands Yacht Club* launch and used considerably as the *"Club Boat."* It is uncertain when *George C. Boldt* obtained the *Crescent* and from whom. *Mr. Boldt* was a member of the *Thousand Islands Yacht Club* as well as serving as Vice-Commodore in 1908.

On July 14, 1917, the *Crescent* was listed on an affidavit of *Mr. Boldt's* boats. It was listed with a value of $2,000.00 at that time.

**Researcher's note:** An article on March 28, 1928 said that while in winter lay up, the *Crescent* sank. She was lying in a small cove to the west of the Ogdensburg lighthouse. Heavy rains plus shifting ice holed her and she went down. The article went on to say that the vessel cost $13,000.00 when new and was owned by *Captain George P. Flemming* when it sank. It is uncertain at this time if this was two different boats with the same name. Another picture of the *Crescent* can be seen on page 38.

CRICKET - was a 24-foot motor boat with a 9 foot beam and had a 24 hp. *Barker* engine. Her speed was 10 miles per hour (see information on *Cocoa*). *George C. Boldt Jr.'s* nickname was *Cricket* and this may have been the boat he used.

DAIRY MAID - * - The motor boat *Dairy Maid* was 20 feet long and had a 4 foot beam. It was appraised on July 14, 1917 for $25.00 and was built around 1900.

BELOW WHAT IS BELIEVED TO BE THE FLAT SCOW *DERRICK #2* AS IT IS TOWED BY THE *FROST KING*. THE SCOW WAS USED FOR CARRYING GOODS AND SUPPLIES TO *MR. BOLDT'S* ISLAND PROPERTIES. HIS *"UNFINISHED"* SUMMER HOME, NOW CALLED *BOLDT CASTLE* ON *HEART ISLAND* IS IN THE BACKGROUND. THIS PHOTOGRAPH WAS TAKEN SOMETIME BEFORE AUGUST 1913. THE *FROST KING* WAS ALSO OWNED BY *MR. BOLDT*.

DERRICK #1 - * - In the working outfit there was the flat scow named *Derrick #1*. It was 40 feet long and had a 16-foot beam. It was listed as 23 tons and built around 1900. It was stated that on July 14, 1917 it required large amounts of repairs and was appraised at $150.00 at that time.

DERRICK #2 - * - This flat scow was 25 feet long with a 12 foot beam and was built around 1896-1897 period. On July 14, 1917 it was listed as greatly out of repair and had an appraised value of $50.00.

DIXIE - * - This little motor boat was built around 1903. Its length was 19 feet and had a 4 and 1/2 -foot beam and powered by a 2 and 1/2 horse power Norwalk engine. Her speed was 10 miles per hour. It was listed as having an appraised value of $25.00 on July 14, 1917.

DREDGE - * - was just that..... a dredge. As part of the working fleet, it was 70 feet long and had a 29-foot beam. It was built in 1897 and by July 1917 it was out of working order and could not be used. On July 14, 1917 appraised value of it was placed at $1,200.00.

ELLEN - * - The flat scow named *Ellen* was part of the working outfit. It was 65 feet long and had a 18 foot beam. Its tonnage was listed as 73 tons. It was built in 1898 and by July 1917 it was badly in need of repair. It was listed as having an appraised value of $250.00 on July 14, 1917.

ETHEL DALE - * - was a motor boat which was built in 1915. It had a length of 30 feet and had a 6-foot beam. It was propelled by gasoline. The appraised value on July 14, 1917 was placed at $1,800.00.

THE FROST KING HEADING OUT INTO THE ST. LAWRENCE RIVER. *MR. BOLDT'S WELLESLEY HOUSE* IS TO THE RIGHT AND HIS MAMMOTH BARN AT THE *FRONT FARM* IS ON THE LEFT

THE *FROST KING* IN FRONT OF *BOLDT'S* MAMMOTH BARN AT HIS *FRONT FARM . MR. BOLDT'S* HELMSMAN FOR THE *FROST KING* WAS *MR. EVARD WAGONER.*

FROST KING - was 30 feet over all and had a 6 foot 6 inch beam. It was powered by a 30 hp. *Jensick* engine which gave her a speed of 16 miles per hour. The *Frost King* was built around 1906 for *George C. Boldt* and on one August 1906 Monday morning it barely escaped being cut in two with two young men on board. It is uncertain if *Evard Wagoner* was one of the young men injured. He would have been 17 years old at the time. He was born in 1888.

A serious accident, imperiling several lives, was narrowly averted by the timely presence of mind of *Captain Visger* of the boat *Idler*. The accident occurred as the *Idler* was coming in to *Cornwall's* dock at Alexandria Bay, New York from her usual morning ramble. Directly in her path and not twenty feet away, lazily lay the *Frost King*, with her two occupants in the cabin starting the engine, unmindful of the loud blast of warning from the approaching yacht. When a collision seemed imminent *Captain Visger* swung the wheel to starboard at the immediate danger of sending his boat into the dock bow on, and barely grazed the prow of the *Frost King*. The crippled boat was towed to shore and the *Idler* continued on her way none the worse for her little brush. As it was the *Frost King* sustained a badly damaged hull, and would be out of commission for some time.

EVARD WAGONER WITH A MEMBER OF _GEORGE C. BOLDT'S_ HOUSEHOLD STAFF

Florence Estelle Dixon taught school on Wellesley Island before she married *Evard Wagoner* on October 22, 1912. He was 24 years old when he married her. During the winter months *Evard* worked on *Mr. Boldt's "back farm"* making butter. He had previously worked at the golf course.

A wedding cake for their very special occasion was made at the *Waldorf-Astoria Hotel* in New York City where *George C. Boldt* was the proprietor of. A letter to *Florence Estelle Dixon*, the future bride was written on *Waldorf-Astoria Hotel* stationary on October 20, 1912 and was from *W.* Atkinson, *George C. Boldt's* butler. It reads:

WEDDING CAKE MADE AT THE WALDORF - ASTORIA HOTEL FOR EVARD & FLORENCE WAGONER

My Dear Miss Dixon,

"Many thanks for your kind letter. Please accept my regrets for I am unable to keep my promise in sending you white flowers for cake. I've tried nearly every large shop I came across, and have failed, at this time of year. There is only colored ones to be got, "I am so sorry." Nevertheless the cake I hope will taste just so sweet. Please find enclosed the best photo I took of it and hope you all like it.. We leave for the Bay tomorrow night. I shall hear all particulars. I hope Evard did not break much of the sugar by the journey. Now please accept my best wishes for your future happiness." Yours very sincerely, W. Atkinson.

Evard Wagoner was only one of the thousands of people that *George C. Boldt* had in his employment. With ownership of the *Bellevue* and *Stratford* hotels, (later the *Bellevue-Stratford Hotel*) in Philadelphia, Pennsylvania and proprietor of the *Waldorf* and *Astoria* hotels in New York City, in addition a huge farm on Wellesley Island, many of these employees found a loyalty and fondness for *Mr. Boldt.* The Thousand Islands had a very special place in the heart and mind of *Mr. Boldt.* The people there may have known him best as he was very concerned for them and there well being.

EVARD WAGONER ABOVE WITH THE *FROST KING*. BELOW THE *FROST KING* IS SHOWN HERE ON THE RIGHT. THE MAN IS *SI VROOMAN* WITH *FLORENCE DIXON WAGONER*

ABOVE THE *FROST KING* WITH *EVARD WAGONER* ON THE LEFT WITH HIS SISTER *IRENA.* HIS SISTER *MIRA* IS IN THE BOAT. HIS SISTER *LENA* IS ON THE RIGHT SITTING WITH A FRIEND. THE PLACE WAS KNOWN AS THE BONDORF'S AND NOW KNOWN AS POINT MARGUERITE WHICH IS OWNED BY THE *RICHARD MCSHERRY* FAMILY

THE *FROST KING* AS IT APPROACHES THE *GEORGE C. BOLDT* ESTATE ON WELLESLEY
ISLAND. THE ISLANDS IMPERIAL AND JUST ROOM ENOUGH IN THE BACKGROUND

SHOWN HERE IN THE BACKGROUND IS THE *FROST KING* MOORED AT *GEORGE C. BOLDT'S* TENNIS ISLAND ESTATE. THE TWO MEN IN THE BOAT ARE UNIDENTIFIED. BELOW AT THE LEFT IS *EVARD WAGONER* WITH A FRIEND. THE BOAT MAY HAVE BEEN THE *GOLF*

YOUNG *EVARD WAGONER* ON A BREZY DAY WITH *BOLDT CASTLE* ON *HEART ISLAND* BEHIND HIM

On July 6, 1913 the motor boat *Frost King* was demolished by *Nathan Straus's* yacht *Sisilina* in the St. Lawrence River near Cherry Island. *Captain Lewis Derian* was the pilot of the *Sisilina*. *Mr. Boldt*, who went back to *The Waldorf Hotel* in New York City from ten days stay at his place in the Thousand Islands said the yacht was in no way at fault, so far as he could learn. Before leaving his country place he had a warrant issued for the arrest of *Orrin Porter*, the man who was running the boat. He said there had been many cases of boatmen stealing their employer's craft and taking out joy riding parties, and that he and the other members of the summer colony have determined to break it up.

Mr. Boldt did not know that anything had happened to his motor boat the *Frost King* until his Italian laborers failed to appear for work on Monday morning. Inquiry showed that they had been marooned at Alexandria Bay ever since Sunday afternoon at 5 o'clock.

"I had two boats, the Frost King and the Frost King II," said *Mr. Boldt*. *"The first had been used as a sort of ferry-boat, to run errands and take care of the workmen's and servants trips to the mainland, and when I was told that this boat had too much work to do, I got a second for the use of the servants alone and turned the older boat over to the back farm. The man Orrin Porter had instructions to take the farm hands over to Alexandria Bay to do their shopping.*

THE *FROST KING* IS SHOWN HERE IN THE FOREGROUND AND *MR. BOLDT'S* STEAM YACHT *LOUISE* IS IN THE BACKGOUND. THE *FROST KING* WAS DEMOLISHED BY THE STEAM YACHT *SISILINA* WHICH WAS ABOUT THE SIZE OF THE *LOUISE*.

"On Sunday the Italian workmen wanted to have a picnic, and the Superintendent told Porter to take them to the island where this was held, and bring them back home by 5 o'clock.

"At that hour nobody appeared, and nobody knew what had become of the boat or workmen. On Monday morning they did not appear, and then we heard that they were waiting over at Alexandria Bay for a chance to get back. It developed that Porter had taken the party from the island late on Sunday afternoon, and landed them at Alexandria Bay. Then telling them that he would be back in a few minutes, he had gone off and taken a party from the Thousand Island House joy riding. He never turned up.

"To my astonishment, the Justice of the Peace told me that Porter had taken the same party out on Friday night, and I learned that the man had been in the habit of doing the same thing for some time. I had a warrant issued for his arrest. There has been an epidemic of this sort of thing up there, and people are determined that it shall stop. For that reason an example will be made of Porter.

"The Straus yacht blew her whistle, but the people on the motor boat were evidently having too much fun to pay attention. The boat was about 5 years old, worth only $500 or $600, but she is a total wreck having been cut into four pieces. Besides the one man who drowned, several of the occupants of the boat were injured. People up there feel that there has been a lot too much of this joy riding going on, and the charge against Porter will be pressed. This is not the first time I have had a boat lost up there."

Captain Lewis Derian the pilot of the *Sisilina* was exonerated of all blame in the collision with the *Frost King* on July 6, 1913.

ABOVE *FROST KING II* AT *GEORGE C. BOLDT'S* "ICE AND SKIFF HOUSE." NOTE THE *CRESCENT* IN THE BACKGROUND. *EVARD WAGONER* IS AT THE HELM WITH *MR. ATKINSON, BOLDT'S* BUTLER BEHIND HIM WITH ONE OF THE HOUSEKEEPERS. BELOW IS BELIEVED TO BE MORE UNIDENTIFIED STAFF

MR. BOLDT'S HELMSMAN FOR THE *FROST KING II* WAS *EVARD WAGONER* SHOWN IN FRONT OF *"THE ICE HOUSE"* WHICH IS ON WELLESLEY ISLAND. *BOLDT CASTLE* ON *HEART ISLAND* CAN BE SEEN IN THE BACKGROUND ON THE LEFT. BELOW THE *FROST KING II* IS HEADING OUT OF ALEXANDRIA BAY. *EDGEWOOD PARK*, NOW KNOWN AS THE *EDGEWOOD RESORT*, IS IN THE BACKGROUND.

FROST KING II - * - In the same *New York Times* article of July 9, 1913, the *Frost King II* is mentioned. The owner of that boat, *Mr. George C. Boldt,* is quoted as saying that the *Frost King II* was used *"for the servants"* transportation to and from the mainland. The *Frost King II* was built in 1909-10 and was 32 feet long. It had a 6 foot 6 inch beam and the hull construction was of wood. It was powered by a 10 hp. *Model* engine giving her a speed of 10 miles per hour. It was appraised on July 14, 1917 for $300.00. In August of 1923 *Mr. Richard Andress* fractured his right arm while cranking the *Frost King II* engine.

GOLF - was a small 22 foot skiff shaped boat with a 4 foot 6 inch beam and had a 4 hp. *Tassey* engine, giving her a speed of 8 miles an hour. See lower picture on page 35. This may have been the 22 foot motor boat *Golf.*

GOVERNOR – was owned by *George C. Boldt Jr.* and was entered in a August, 1906 motor boat race under the auspices of the *Thousand Islands Yacht Club.* The race was held to see what boats were qualified to represent the *Thousand Islands Yacht Club* in the races for the *Gold Challenge Cup* of the *American Power Boat Association.* The races were for boats with 2 horse power or under.

Entered for the race was *Breese* owned by *Gilbert T. Rafferty; P. D. Q.* owned by *George C. Boldt Sr.* and raced by his daughter *Louise Clover Boldt; Governor* owned by *George C. Boldt Jr.; Ina* owned by *A. T. Hagan; So Long II* owned by *Stephen Bonsal Jr.; Pirate* owned by *Clarence N. Peacock; Joe Gish* owned by *Ernest Serrell; Sirocco* owned by *Isaac P. Wiser; Pixie* owned by *George S. Hasbrouck;* and *Got-To-Go* owned by *William B. Hayden.* The course was three times around Whiskey Island for a total of 20 and 7/8th miles.

HEART – *George C. Boldt* naphtha launch *Heart* was the fastest of its size in the Thousand Islands in 1898.

BELOW WHAT IS BELIEVED TO BE THE NAPHTHA LAUNCH CALLED *HEART* AS IT HEADS FOR WELLESLEY ISLAND. IN THE BACKGROUND IS *BOLDT CASTLE* ON *HEART ISLAND* WITH AN UNKNOW BOAT MOORED THERE

ABOVE WHAT MIGHT HAVE BEEN THE NAPHTHA LAUNCH CALLED *HEART* AT THE *HEART ISLAND* BOAT HOUSE LANDING. THIS PAINTING WAS DONE BY FRANK H. TAYLOR

KO KO – was a boat owned by *Alfred Graham Miles*, husband of Louise *Clover Boldt Miles*, only daughter of *George C. Boldt*. In 1912 *Alfred Graham Miles* was a member of the *Chippewa Yacht Club*, which was at Chippewa Bay, New York in the Thousand Islands. A boat he owned at that time was the *Ko Ko* which was a *One Design Sloop* which had a length of 26 feet 9 inches at the O. A. At the water line it was 16 feet 3 inches and had a beam of 6 feet 6 inches.

The *Chippewa Yacht Club* was organized in 1895. Other members of the club were: J. W. Allison, Hon. Jos. Aspinall, S. G. Averell, Dr. F. R. Bailey, R. H. Barrett, Horace A. Beale, Jr, Walter H. Beebe, W. M. Beers, George F. Benson, George C. Boldt, George C. Boldt, Jr. Arthur K. Bourne, Frederick G. Bourne, Howard Bourne, Edson Bradley, Frank P. Bronson, A. T. Brown, F. K. Burnham, Sam E. Brown, Edward Stephenson Burke, Jr., Dr. E. E. Campbell, C. S. Cossitt, J. E. Chrysler, M. T. Clark, Alfred Costello, Charles W. Crossmon, George F. Darrow, Julian T. Davies, James Doig, J. Frank Dow, R. H. Eggleston, Charles G. Emery, and C. M. Englis, John Englis II, John Englis, Clarence L. Fabre, Fredrick Frazier, H. S. Gillespie, T. A. Gillespie, Dr. J. M. Gibbons, Arthur Gotthold, F. T. Graves, Hon. George Hall, Dr. W. B. Hanbidge, Hon. John Hannan, George S. Hasbrouck, Hon. E. B. Hawkins, C. H. Hayden, C. Leverett Hayden, William B. Hayden, N. A. Heath, William W. Henshaw, E. R. Holden, John C. Howard, J. W. Jackson, L. A. Johnson, Edward M. Kennedy, Willis Sharp Kilmer, Ira Kipp, James G. Knap, M. J. Lawrence. Dr. Egbert LeFevre, Captain D. H. Lyon, Charles McDonald, Price McKinney, Arthur E. Miller, W. D. Morris, Robert Mulford, James T. Murphy, E. R. Nichols, W. H. Nichols, E. A. Oliver, Mrs. Calvin B. Orcutt, James Pass, Alexander R. Peacock, C. N. Peacock, William H. Post, A. B. Quarrier, Frederick A. Reed, J. B. Reid, H. A. Richardson, Alex Robb, H. P. Rose, E. B. Rubsamen, Lee Rumsey, A. D. Seaver, Ernest Serrell, William I. Serrell, R. C. Seymour, Charles E. Sheldon, George G. Sherman, Hon. Clifford Sifton, S. W. Smith, Eben Stephens, E. L. Strong, Dr. William H. Taylor, S. S. Thompson, S. H. Vandergrift, J. Wainwright Jr., Thomas H. Wheeler, and Isaac P. Wiser

LADUCHESSE - * - One of the most luxurious vessels in *George C. Boldt's* fleet of watercraft was the 104 foot houseboat *LaDuch-*

esse. It was designed by the architectural firm of *Tams, LaMoine and Crane*, of New York City. The original plan was to build the boat there, but was built by the *Dravo Corporation* of Philadelphia, Pennsylvania. After constructed it was to be towed to Alexandria Bay, New York via the Erie Barge Canal. However, this plan was abandoned when a member of the staff realized that the completed boat would not pass under the bridges spanning the canal.

Mr. Boldt, a determined man, insisted on his original design appearing on the St. Lawrence River. It was then that it was decided to build the boat in sections, ship it by rail to Clayton, New York, and then scow the sections to the *Boldt* estate on Wellesley Island for final assembly.

Built in 1903 and registered as vessel No. 162418, the *LaDuchesse* had a net tonnage of 247. Her length was 104 feet and width was 21 feet and depth was 4 feet 3 inches. Her all mahogany hull and two story living quarters make her a luxury floating summer home. The original construction cost of the boat was $175,000.00.

LADUCHESSE

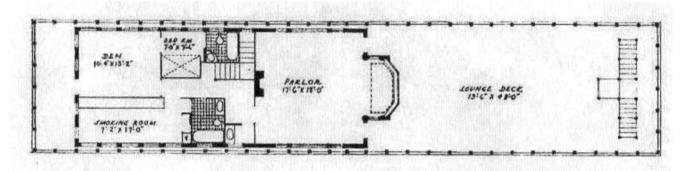

ABOVE THE UPPER DECK OF *GEORGE C. BOLDT'S* HOUSEBOAT *LADUCHESSE.*
BELOW IS THE LOWER DECK

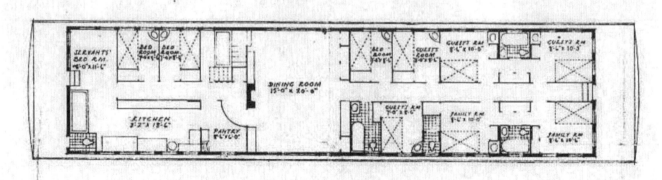

FROM THESE RIVER SCENE'S, *MR. BOLDT'S* 104 FOOT HOUSEBOAT *LADUCHESS* IS AT THE CANAL ENTRANCE ON THE RIGHT IN FRONT OF *MR. BOLDT'S WELLESLEY HOUSE* WHICH WAS PART OF HIS *FRONT FARM.* THE *"ICE AND SKIFF HOUSE"* IS TO THE LEFT, AND THE STEAM TUG *QUEEN* IS AT THE FAR RIGHT OF THE LOWER PHOTOGRAPH. HIS YACHT HOUSE WAS DOWN STREAM (TO THE RIGHT) OF THESE PICTURES

The upper deck consisted of a 19 feet 6 inch by 48 foot lounge deck, a 17 feet 6 inch by 18 foot parlor, a 10 feet 4 inch by 13 feet 2 inch den, a 7 foot 2 inch by 17 foot smoking room, a 7 foot by 7 foot 6 inch bedroom, and two bathrooms.

ABOVE IS THE *LADUCHESSE* BEING TOWED BY *BOLDT'S* STEAM TUG *QUEEN.* THE *LADUCHESSE* NEVER WAS EQUIPPED WITH POWER AND WAS ALWAYS TOWED FROM PLACE TO PLACE. NOTE THE OPEN *"DANCING DECK"* ON THE UPPER LEVEL

LADUCHESSE AT THE *THOUSAND ISLANDS YACHT CLUB* ON WELCOME ISLAND. BELOW TO THE LEFT IS THE *LADUCHESSE* AT THE *THOUSAND ISLAND CLUB.* ON THE RIGHT IS THE YACHT *CLOVER.* THE "T. I. CLUB" AS IT IS OFTEN REFERRED TO, PLAYED HOST TO MANY GALA EVENTS. BOATING PARTIES USED THE FACILITY FOR THEIR DINING AND DANCING PLEASURE, AS WELL AS A PLACE FOR LODGING.

EXCITING EVENTS AT THE ST. LAWRENCE RIVER ARE BOAT RACES. SHOWN HERE IS THE HOUSEBOAT *LADUCHESSE* MOORED AT *ALSTER TOWER* ON *HEART ISLAND*. SMOKE TO THE RIGHT OF IT IS FROM THE STEAM TUG *QUEEN* WHICH TOWED IT FROM PLACE TO PLACE. *BOLDT'S* DAUGHTER *LOUISE CLOVER* AND HUSBAND *ALFRED GRAHAM MILES* WERE BOTH VERY ACTIVE IN BOAT RACING.

This vessel is one of the most unique vessels in the world and features an original *Tiffany* glass skylight, gold leaf stenciling, bronze and marble fireplaces, and mahogany cabin accommodations. The *LaDuchesse* boasts a deck for dancing, quarters for family and servants, two open fireplaces and awnings to raise and lower in accordance with the weather. It has steel bulkheads, steam heat, eleven bedrooms, seven baths, dining room and salon. It was fully equipped and furnished including silver, glass and linen.

The lower deck consisted of a 15 foot by 20 foot dining room, a 8 foot 2 inch by 18 foot 6 inch kitchen, a 8 foot 6 inch by 6 foot pantry, 2 family bedrooms measuring 8 foot 6 inch by 10 feet and 8 foot 6 inch by 10 foot 6 inch, also guest bedrooms measuring 8 feet 6 inch by 10 feet, another at 8 feet 6 inches by 10 feet 3 inches, another 8 feet by 8 feet 6 inches and a fourth one at 7 feet by 8 feet 6 inches. A servants' bedroom at 6 feet by 11 feet 6 inches and 3 other bedrooms ranging in sizes of 7 feet by 8 feet 4 inches. There were 5 bathrooms on the lower deck.

THE LOUNGE OR DANCING DECK OF THE *LADUCHESSE* IN 1908 MEASURES 17 ' - 6" BY 49 FEET. THIS OPEN DECK PROVIDES MUCH ENJOYMENT. BELOW AS IT LOOKS TODAY.

THE PARLOR OF THE *LADUCHESSE* IN 1908 ABOVE AND TODAY BELOW. NOTE THE
BEAUTIFUL STEINWAY PIANO WITH *TIFFANY* SKYLIGHT ABOVE IT

THIS VIEW OF THE *LADUCHESSE'S* PARLOR IN AUGUST 1908. *MR. BOLDT* ALWAYS HAD IT ADORNED WITH FRESH CUT FLOWERS FROM HIS GARDENS. NOTE THE BEAUTIFUL *STEINWAY* PIANO AT THE RIGHT. BELOW IS THE FIREPLACE AS IT LOOKS TODAY.

THIS 1908 PHOTO SHOWS THE LOWER LEVEL OF THE *LADUCHESSE* IN THE DINING ROOM WITH A *TIFFANY* LAMP AND BRASS STUDDED FIREPLACE WITH SEA SHELLS. AT RIGHT THE FIREPLACE AS IT LOOKS TODAY. BELOW SOME OF THE ORIGINAL *GEORGE C. BOLDT* DISHES ABOARD THE *LADUCHESSE*

A 1905 VIEW OF THE *LADUCHESSE* MOORED AT THE *BOLDT YACHT HOUSE. ALSTER TOWER* AND *ARCH OF HONOR* ON HEART ISLAND IS IN THE FOREGROUND

THE *LADUCHESSE* ON THE RIGHT OF THE *BOLDT YACHT HOUSE*

AN EARLY VIEW OF *GEORGE C. BOLDT'S* 104 FOOT HOUSEBOAT *LADUCHESSE*

There are some things, which once tried, become a habit and house boating is one of them. While the houseboat is an ancient craft, its great allurement is found in the ease with which it may be moved from point to point without the least inconvenience. To derive the most benefit from frequent moves, the places visited each must be possessed of individual charm to maintain interest and afford variety of scenery. Hence it is among the Thousand Islands that house boating is at its best.

George C. Boldt took every advantage of seeing and sharing the St. Lawrence River with family and friends with his houseboat. The *LaDuchesse* could be anchored off the *Thousand Island Club* or *Thousand Islands Yacht Club*, but as a rule was made fast to a sea wall near the Tennis House location, thus securing electric light and water connections, and accessibility to golf, tennis and polo. Since its first days, *LaDuchesse* has always been replete with fresh flowers, from the brightly colored window boxes, which decorate her rails, to the beautiful centerpieces of her deck-side tables.

Mr. James H. Hutchinson listed the *LaDuchesse* as having an appraised value of $12,000.00 on July 14, 1917.

By 1918 the *Boldt* family rented out the *LaDuchesse* at $100.00 per day. It was advertised in the *Town and Country Magazine*. The service of a pilot was included in the rental. As many as twelve to fourteen could be cared for on this houseboat, fully furnished, linen, silver, glassware, etc., included. In 1919 the rental income from the *LaDuchesse* was $1,600.00. The *LaDuchesse* was well cared for with her all mahogany hull and luxurious furnishings kept in best of repair. But like story-book royalty, she was pampered in her early life and then went through a period of hard times.

Mr. Edward John Noble purchased the late *George C. Boldt Sr.'s* estate in the early 1920's and the deal included the title to the *LaDuchesse*. It was after this time that the *LaDuchesse* suffered a period of decline. *The Thousand Islands Yacht Club* on Welcome Island was discontinued in the 1930's and the *LaDuchesse* was elected to serve as a temporary club headquarters for die-hard members of the club. This use was eventually abandoned and the houseboat was relegated to storage in the *Boldt Yacht House* bay, which was constructed for her in 1905. It was used for a time by members of the *Thousand Islands Yacht Club* when it abandoned its' club house on Welcome Island.

It was during this period that the boat suffered the most ignominious blow of a long career. Simple neglect and not pumping and laying up the closet outlets sank her. In addition, when she did sink, the bottom was penetrated by 2 old piles nobody seemed to know were there. It appeared that she was finished since *Mr. Noble* was apparently exasperated and did not seem inclined to float her again.

LOWER DECK HALL LEADING TO THE BEDROOMS & BATHROOMS

***BOLDT* CREST IS ON ALL THE DOORKNOBS**

MR. ANDREW McNALLY III

Ownership of the houseboat *LaDuchesse* was obtained from *Mr. Edward J. Noble* by *Mr. Andrew McNally III* of Island Royal and Evanston, Illinois. This transaction took place in 1943. *Mr. McNally* purchased the *LaDuchesse* from *Mr. Noble* for $1.00. *Mr. Andrew McNally III* was Chairman of *Rand McNally* mapmakers and his family had summer homes on Wellesley Island. His parents brought him to the St. Lawrence River when he *"was 3 weeks old and put him in the river."* This began a lifetime of devotion to the Thousand Islands region.

Andrew McNally III succeeded his father as president of *Rand McNally and Company* in 1948. His father was *Andrew F. McNally* and was also chairman of the board of *Rand, McNally and Company*. He died on May 20, 1954 after a short illness. His father had founded the firm in 1856. *Andrew F. McNally* had been associated with the business since 1907.

Mr.Andrew McNally III had the partially submerged *LaDuchesse* raised from its location at the *Boldt Yacht House* and had the boat put into shape for his personal use. *Mr. Perry Hazelwood*, a diver from Thousand Island Park on Wellesley Island, was engaged in doing the underwater patching on the hull and plumbing system, and *Charles Garlock and Sons* from Alexandria Bay, New York, were in charge of the repair work. *Mr. Hazelwood* said *"Much of the furniture and rugs had been covered with water. The handsomely finished woodwork had been discolored by water and where veneer was used, the surface had been warped."*

In a letter from *H. L. Rafferty* of 155 E. 73rd Street, New York City, tells about the raising of the *LaDuchesse.*

"The houseboat raising was really interesting and not of which Clarence and the diver did 9/10ths and I am enclosing some pictures of it at various stages including the Clayton fire engine pumping from a scow. Also the village fire boat and Chiefs' car. It was a joy to watch the big pump from Syracuse, which you'll note on the 2nd deck. 5 in all did the job and she came up quite gracefully.

"There was practically no furniture downstairs, but stove and icebox retained are in excellent condition. Most of the damage was to the less expensively built walls in the servant's quarters but it would seem that a couple of carpenters plus a couple of painters in 2 weeks time could make everything quite livable, that is if the children do not wish the tedious, expensive job of having the interior scraped and revarnished, instead of painting. Luckily the ceiling, with many difficult interstices between the many beams, were not reached by the water and are in perfect condition while only 1 of the 2 large dining room windows was broken. All, even the small ones, are heavy plate glass.

"No trouble getting the boat up to her final moorings and she towed so fast and easily. The only rot in her was where air and water meet. The bottom is sound and wood always under water rarely rots"

In October of 1946 the houseboat *LaDuchesse* was towed by the *Edith II* and *Gloria II,* large touring boats of the *Thousand Islands Yacht Line, Inc.* of Clayton, New York, to the *Canadian Dredge and Dock Company* of Kingston, Ontario, Canada for repairs and modernizing. The work was done in their dry dock. Then in May of 1947 the *Edith II* and *Gloria II* brought it back to Wellesley Island estate to be used as a summer home for the *McNally* family.

The houseboat *LaDuchesse* was towed again in 1957 so a new steel hull could replace the wooden hull. The new hull was designed by Mr. *Glenn Furness* and the steel for it came from Chicago, Illinois.

The contract for the construction was awarded to *Hutchinson Boat Works, Incorporated* of Alexandria Bay, New York. Work on the new hull was done at the company's Holland Street yards of the boat works. The new hull, which replaced the original wood structure under the living quarters, cost in the neighborhood of $50,000.00. The new hull is 106 feet long with a 26-foot beam and a depth of 5 feet.

Mr. Andrew McNally III and his wife, the former *Miss Margaret Clark McMillian*, had 3 children, *Betty Jane, Andrew McNally IV (Sandy),* and *Edward (Ted) Clark McNally,* who all enjoyed living aboard the *LaDuchesse* for many years. Their love, devotion, and interest in the Thousand Island region was shared with their guests who enjoyed many happy occasions aboard this palatial vessel. It proved to be the ideal place to enjoy a quality of life that provided a lifetime of memories.

Mrs. Margaret Clark McNally passed away and with her 3 children grown up with families of their own, a new generation of *McNally* family members were added and became the proud legacy to enjoy the *LaDuchesse* and the dynamic St. Lawrence River. *Andrew McNally IV (Sandy)* became president of *Rand McNally and Company* in 1974. He was 34 years old and represented the fifth generation of *McNallys* to head the company. It was in that year that his father, *Andrew McNally III* became chairman of the board.

As a devoted trustee of the *Thousand Islands Shipyard Museum,* (now called the *Antique Boat Museum*) in Clayton, New York, from 1979 to 1995, a period of 16 years, *Mr. Andrew McNally III* had showed great leadership and guidance to this now world renowned organization. His support, interest, and contributions of time, effort, energy, as well as funding, have enriched the museum in the preserving the vast nautical history of the St. Lawrence River. It should be noted here that *Mr. Clarence Manue* was caretaker for Mr. McNally, and Mrs. Nancy Bond was his housekeeper.

In 1986, *Mr. Andrew McNally III* announced that he was donating the houseboat *LaDuchesse* to the *Antique Boat Museum.* The museum had been in the process of preparing a place for this most generous gift. Before the *LaDuchesse* came to the *Antique Boat Museum,* there would be an infrastructure and an endowment that is commensurate with the vessels elegance. The *Long Range Planning Committee* had been working closely with *Grater Architectures* to develop the proper site docks and gardens for the *LaDuchesse.*

To further ensure the prime maintenance of the *LaDuchesse,* it was taken again to Kingston, Ontario, Canada in 1996 for bottom repairs. *Junior Rusho* provided tugs for this move, which was supervised by *Ken Johnson.*

The very kind, generous, and compassionate *Andrew McNally III* passed away on November 15, 2001 at his winter home in Chicago, Illinois. He was 92 years old and had enjoyed owning the *LaDuchesse* for 58 years. *Mr. McNally* was greatly admired, respected, and loved by family and friends, of which he had many. He is to this day sadly missed, but fondly remembered by this author.

The *LaDuchesse* was moved from the *McNally* compound on Wellesley Island on May 7, 2005 to the *Antique Boat Museum* in Clayton, New York. An official opening of this historic and beautiful houseboat was given on July 2, 2005. Now the general public is the invited guest to enjoy a tour of this magnificent and historical vessel.

Carrying on a tradition of support, concern, and assistance to the *Antique Boat Museum* the *McNally* family members contribute much of their time and talents to this fine institution in preserving and maintaining its huge collection. Society is the beneficiary to such vision and foresight. Applause to them all with a heart felt *"thank you."*

THE *LOUISE* AT THE CENTER BAY OF THE *BOLDT YACHT HOUSE.* THE *LADUCHESSE* IS AT THE LEFT OF THE VERY ELEGANT 102 FOOT STEAM/SAILING YACHT *LOUISE*

Editors note: According to the book *The Waldorf-Astoria: America's Gilded Dream* by *Ward Morehouse III*, (1991) he states that Oscar Tschirky *"invented, or had concocted for him, (Boldt), what all the world knows today as the apple-filled Waldorf Salad"* aboard the *LaDuchesse*. This is unconfirmed as yet, to be true. More pictures of the *LaDuchesse* can be seen on page 5, 6, 7, and on the back cover.

The *Antique Boat Museum* contains the finest collection of historic freshwater boats and engines in North America. Over 200 examples of small craft, marine engines and related objects in the museum's collection reflects the rich nautical heritage of the Thousand Islands region. The museum's library and archives contain an extensive collection of books and periodicals related to nautical history and the St. Lawrence River.

A visit to the *Antique Boat Museum* at 750 Mary Street in Clayton, New York (zip code 13624) is a very rewarding experience for all ages. Not going to this fine museum while at the Thousand Islands is like going to *Egypt* and not seeing the *Pyramids*. The museum is a must see place of enjoyment, pleasure, education and history! It is open from mid-May to mid-October each year. Their web address is www.abm.org. or call at 315- 686- 4104. Their fax number is 315-686-2775.

LADY PAT – was owned by *Louise Clover Boldt Miles,* only daughter of *George C. Boldt*, and wife of *Alfred Graham Miles*. No data on this boat is available yet.

LOUISE * - The very elegant yacht *Louise* was a combination steam and sailing yacht and was designed and built by the *Herreshoff Manufacturing Company* at *Bristol, Rhode Island* in 1893. Construction was wood. Her specifications were as follows: net 24 tons, gross tons, 49; over all length, 102 feet; waterline length, 84 feet. Her beam was 14 feet; depth 8 feet 2 inches; draft 4 feet 4 inches. Her power plant was a 3 cylinder triple expansion steam engine, 5 and 5/8 inch, 9 and 14 by 9 which was also built at the *Herreshoff* plant. On each side of the boiler were coal bunkers. Above the engine room was a skylight. There were 18 portholes in all, 9 on each side of the vessel.

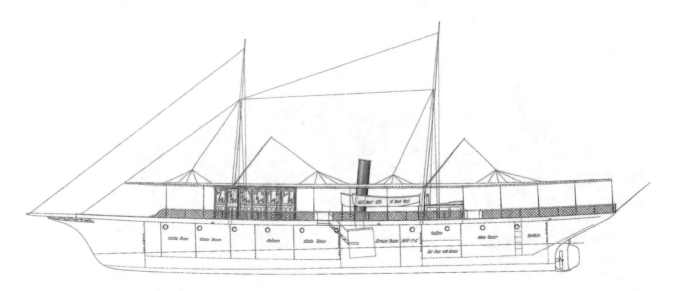

GEORGE C. BOLDT'S 102 FOOT STEAM YACHT LOUISE HAD A BATH TUB IN IT

The steam yacht *Louise* had 11 iron bulkheads. Below deck it had 3 staterooms, a saloon, engine room, a galley which had a stove and icebox. Then there was a mess room and captain's quarters. Behind the captain's quarters was room for storage. The mess room and crew quarters contained 3 settee berths and 2 lockers. A ladder provided access to a hatch and deck above. The galley also had access to a hatch above.

In the forward end of the *Louise,* with its clipper bow, was the chain room for the anchor. Behind this area was a clothes room then the first state room. In it were a bed with drawers underneath, a wash basin, and a settee. The second state room also had a bed with drawers underneath and a settee berth. This room had a toilet room on the port side and a locker opposite it on the starboard side. A saloon and the third state room were next. On each side of this room were beds that would extend a wash basin on each side, and a bathtub in the center. The beds had drawers underneath. There also were folding doors in the center of this room.

On the top deck was a saloon and dining room. Settee areas were on each side with doors on the aft end that led to the main deck. A stairway on the forward end of this room led to the staterooms on the deck below. The forward and after-end bulkheads of the pilot house were covered in 1 and 1/8 inch mahogany. The pilothouse measured 8 feet 2 and 1/2 inches by 6 feet 4 and 1/8 inches. On the main deck were 2 lifeboats. The one on the starboard side measured 14 feet 3 inches and the one on the port side measured 12 feet.

In July 1893 this superb new pleasure yacht appeared at the Thousand Islands. It was captained by *Louis Derrian* and *A. P. Combs* was the engineer. The steam yacht *Louise* belonged to *Mr. Charles H. Hayden* of Columbus, Ohio and Fairyland Island, Alexandria Bay, New York at that time.

It is uncertain when *Mr. Boldt* obtained the *Louise,* but would state it was around 1901. The homeport was listed as Alexandria Bay, New York and the port of registry was Cape Vincent, New York, when *Mr. Boldt* owned the vessel.

One Saturday in August of 1902 *George* and *Louise Boldt* took a party of 24 young people on their beautiful steam yacht *Louise* to the *Gananoque Inn* in the picturesque village of *Gananoque, Ontario, Canada.* Situated on the mighty St. Lawrence River in the Thousand Islands, the *Gananoque Inn* hosted a *Midsummer Ball Masque,* which was the crowning event for this popular place.

Electricity was called on to transform the grounds of the hotel and Squaw Point where it is located, into a veritable fairy bower, and the myriad of colored lights twinkling among the trees, and the hotel ablaze with electric lighted Japanese lanterns, was a sight not soon to be forgotten.

Young people from Brockville, Ontario, Canada were brought by *Mr.* and *Mrs. Comstock.* From Kingston, Ontario, Canada came a party of 20 aboard the *Mine-ha-ha* from the *Kingston Yacht Club.* Others were *Colonel* and *Mrs. C. H. Drury* and party from Helenbosch, *Dr.* and *Mrs. Atkinson* from *Belle Isle,* and *Mr.* and *Mrs. William Allen* chaperoning 10 young ladies from Bogg's Island. There were others from many of the neighboring islands.

THE *GANANOQUE INN* AT GANANOQUE, ONTARIO, CANADA

When *Professor Begg's* orchestra struck up the opening march, fully two hundred young people in costume of bewildering beauty invaded the dancing floor. Princes, dukes and barbarian kings mingled with flower girls, clowns, rough riders, and even his satanic majesty, and seldom even at a city function were so many beautiful dresses displayed.

At 10:30 p.m. everyone was unmasked and at 11:00 pm a buffet supper was served in the main dining room, after which dancing was continued until midnight. It was whispered around the hotel that the clock was moved back several times.

Among the elaborate decorations of the parlors were pictures of *King Edward* and *President Roosevelt* draped in the English and American flags, in honor of *Coronation Day*. At the end of the dance the orchestra struck up *"God Save The King"* and the entire assemblage, as with one accord, joined in and sang the verse through, after which three rousing cheers were given for the newly crowned King, a hearty tribute from an American gathering. The evening at the *Gananoque Inn* proved to be one of the most brilliant and successful entertainments ever given on the river and reflected great credit on the management who spared no pains or expense to afford their guests and their visitors a delightful evening.

"THE LEGEND OF THE THOUSAND ISLAND DRESSING."

There are different *"versions"* as to how the *Thousand Island Dressing* originated. The most popular known, and believed to be the most accurate, is that it was *George C. Boldt*, of the famous *Boldt Castle* that named it *"Thousand Island Dressing."* Legend has it that it was aboard *Mr. Boldt's* steam yacht *Louise* that his steward created the dressing while sailing on the St. Lawrence River one afternoon. As you have read, and as a reminder, *George C. Boldt* was the proprietor of the world famous *Waldorf* and *Astoria* hotels in New York City, and the owner and proprietor of the equally world famous *Bellevue* and *Stratford* hotels in Philadelphia, Pennsylvania.

It was at *George C. Boldt's* establishments where *Thousand Island Dressing* would be served. Naming the popular dressing after the Thousand Island region was his way of advertising the area he greatly loved and enjoyed immensely, and wanted to share this with his thousands of patrons.

THE 102 FOOT STEAM YACHT *LOUISE* AND *"THE LEGEND OF THE THOUSAND ISLAND DRESSING."* NOTE THE CHEF IN THE CENTER WITH TRADITIONAL ATTIRE.

Legend has it that the steward was *"Oscar of the Waldorf."* Research on this proves that *"Oscar of the Waldorf"* was *Oscar Tschirky* who was *Maitre d' Hotel* of the *Waldorf-Astoria Hotel*, <u>and never a chef</u>. This is stated by him in the book *Oscar of the Waldorf* by *Karl Schriftgiesser* and published by *E. P. Dutton & Co., Inc.,* 1943. As *Mr. Boldt's "right-hand-man"* for 26 years, *Oscar* became very wealthy in his own right and no proof has been found to date that he was ever at the Thousand Islands.

Another claim to the creation of the *Thousand Island Dressing* was a chef at Chicago's *Blackstone Hotel* who named it *Blackstone Dressing*, then renamed it *Thousand Island Dressing*. Still another claim is that it was created by *Mrs. George LaLonde* who worked in the kitchen of the *Harold House* in Clayton, New York, at the turn of the century. She was also employed by the famous actress, *Mae Irwin*, friend of *George C. Boldt*. In October, 1904, Mae Irwin produced a cookbook which was published by the *Frederick A. Stokes Company,* and printed by the *University Press*, Cambridge, Massachusetts. She states the recipes in her book as from chefs, waiters and others. The *Thousand Island Dressing* was not included in that publication.

A picture on *Thousand Island Inn* bottle of *Original Thousand Islands Dressing* with *Mrs. LaLonde* on it reads that she created it *"for her husband who was a noted fishing guide, who served it to his parties as part of his popular shore dinners."* Good for him! Also on the label is a picture of the *Thousand Island Inn,* which claims to be the *"first dining establishment in the world to offer its guests the only salad dressing ever named for a region of the United States."* <u>This author has enjoyed eating there many times!</u>

To add an international flair to the creation of the *Thousand Island Dressing, CBC* of Canada related how the dressing came to be in a *"Culture Shock"* segment that was filmed in 2002. *Hal McCarney*, owner of the *Gananoque Boat Line* from Gananoque, Ontario, Canada told the *Oscar of the Waldorf* story. The video *CBC* did claim that the *Thousand Island Dressing* was a *"Canadian original,"* and made culinary history. And so it goes.

The *Kraft* food people do not know where they obtained their recipe for *Thousand Island Dressing*. Their archive department at *Morton Grove, Illinois* was one of the many sources that this researcher/author has contacted. If a picture is *"worth a thousand words"* then the one of the steam yacht *Louise* with the chef on board certainly supports the creation of the *Thousand Island Dressing* aboard *Mr. Boldt's* beautiful steam yacht *Louise*. Who the steward was will take more research.

Original   **Kraft**   **Legendary**
Thousand Island Dressing

The photo here shows 3 *"manufacturers"* of this delightful topping. In the center is one of the most recognized by millions of people from around the world. The bottle on the left is 1 of 5,000 per year produced by the *Thousand Island Inn* at Clayton, New York, labeled as *"Original Thousand Island Dressing."*

On the right of the photograph is the *"Legendary Thousand Island Dressing"* which is the *"brain child"* of Canadian promoter of the Thousand Island Region, *Ms. Michelle Caron*. Packaged as a souvenir item for the millions of residents and visitors to the area, this delightful item sports a beautiful drawing of *George C. Boldt's* steam yacht *Louise* as it glides through the waters of the mighty St. Lawrence River. Its label includes some of the following:

As mysteriously as the creator of the *Thousand Island Dressing* is and exactly where and when it was first served will take much more time to get to the bottom of the jar, bowl, or whatever it was originally served in. In the meantime ingredients for the *Thousand Island Dressing* producers are just as diverse as are the *"legends."* Bear in mind that legends are, according to the dictionary, *"a story or body of stories handed down for generations and popularly regarded as history."*

Original Thousand Island Dressing

Soybean oil, partially hydrogenated soybean oil, whole eggs, vinegar, tomatoes, cucumbers, corn syrup, water, egg yolks, red peppers, salt, dehydrated onions, modified food starch, horseradish, garlic powder, spices, xanthan, gum, sugar, lemon juice, natural flavors, dis-odium EDTA added to protect flavor, sodium benzoate and potassiumsorbate added as preservatives. For authenticity, top each salad and dressing with 1 tablespoon of chopped hard-boiled eggs prior to serving.

Kraft Thousand Island Dressing

Tomato puree (water, tomato paste), high fructose corn syrup, soybean oil, vinegar, chopped pickles, salt, contains less than 2% of egg yolks, modified food starch, water, dried onions, xanthan gum, polysorbate 60, phosphoric acid, spice, artificial color, mustard flour, with potassium sorbate and calcium disodium EDTA as preservatives, guar gum, natural flavor, oleoresin turmeric, yellow 5.

Legendary Thousand Islands Dressing

This world class legend label list of ingredients are: water, canola oil, sugar, diced cucumber, white spirit vinegar, tomato paste, modified corn starch, frozen egg yolk, spices, salt, mustard flour, hydrolyzed plant protein, chives, locust bean gum, dehydrated onions, calcium disodium EDTA to retard oxidation. A portion of the proceeds of this fine dressing go to UNICEF, United Nations Children's Fund. Net contents are 11.8 fluid ounces.

Thousand Island Dressing list of ingredients:

1 quart of mayonnaise, 1/2 cup of chopped olives, 3/4 cup of sweet relish, 1/4 cup of vinegar, 3 hard boiled eggs, 1/4 cup of Worcestershire, dash of ground cloves, 1/2 cup diced red, pepper, 1 tablespoon of sugar

Thousand Island Dressing list of ingredients:

1 cup of mayonnaise, 1 tsp. chopped olives, 3 tbsp. Chili sauce, 1 tsp. Chopped pimento, 1 chopped hard boiled egg, 1 tsp. Chopped chives, 1 tsp. Chopped green pepper, salt and pepper, Mix ingredients, chill and serve over salad. Makes 4 servings

As this author has been researching this material and the life and times of *George C. Boldt* since 1977, one thing I've learned for sure. You can not fabricate history! Documentation is factual proof. Not everything I've come across has to be credited to *Mr. Boldt*, whom I highly regard as a remarkable person! But as the saying goes, *"a picture is worth a thousand words,"* then the one of *Mr. Boldt's* steam yacht *Louise* with his steward on board certainly supports the legend that the *Thousand Island Dressing* was named by him while sailing on the St. Lawrence River one afternoon.

The steam yacht *Louise* was reported as being re-planked in 1911. *George C. Boldt* was a member of the *Chippewa Yacht Club* at Chippewa Bay, New York in the Thousand Islands and the *Louise* was listed in their 1912 directory.

After *Mr. Boldt's* death in 1916, the *Louise* was appraised by *Mr. James H. Hutchinson*. He valued the Louise at $5,000.00 on July 14, 1917. *Mr. Chrows Klock* was at one time the captain of the *Louise*. The *Louise* was listed for rent along with the *Clover* and the *LaDuchesse* in 1918. Rental fees collected in 1919 for the *Louise* alone was $1,600.00.

In the early 1920's the *Louise* left the Thousand Island region and became the property of *Mr. Edwin Delay Burge*. Santa Ana, California became the homeport with Los Angeles, California as port of registry. More pictures of the *Louise* can be seen in on pages 4, 5, 37, 55, and on the back cover.

MARY - * - A flat scow named *Mary* was 65 feet long and had a 16 foot beam. As part of *George C. Boldt's* working fleet, the *Mary's* tonnage was listed as 73 tons. It was built in 1898 and by 1917 it was badly in need of repair. The *Mary* was listed as having a value of $250.00 on the July 14, 1917 appraisal done by *Mr. James H. Hutchinson*.

THE BOAT BELOW IS BELIEVED TO BE THE *M.A.B.* AND WAS OWNED BY *ESTELLE BOLDT*, SHOWN AT THE RIGHT. SHE WAS THE WIFE OF *GEORGE C. BOLDT JR.* THE MAN ON THE DOCK IS *RAY ROGERS* AT HIS MARINA IN ALEXANDRIA BAY

M.A.B - One of the social events *George C. Boldt Jr.* was involved with was held in July of 1919 when his wife *Estelle* gave a party at their summer villa, *The Birches* on Wellesley Island, Alexandria Bay, New York. The event was held to christen her new cruiser, *M.A.B.* The boat was a 25 mile an hour cruiser equipped with a *Van Blerck* engine. The guest included *Captain H. M. Reid, Edgar A. Sierck, Walter Merrali, Mr.* and *Mrs. Ewing L. Rafferty, Mrs. J. Raymond Ellis,* and *Mr.* and *Mrs. J. Norris Oliphant* of New York City. After the christening, *Mrs. Boldt* took her friends for a cruise on her new boat. The *M.A.B.* was one of the handsomest cruisers on the river.

THE *P. D. Q.* **WITH** *MR. BOLDT.* **THE HELMSMAN IS BELIEVED TO BE** *FRED W. ADAMS*

P.D.Q. - (*Pretty Dam Quick*), was built in 1904 by the *Ogdensburgh Boat Company* for *Mr. George C. Boldt.* As a racing boat, it has a long slim cigar shaped hull made of wood. It is 39 feet long and the beam is 4 feet 6 inches. *Mr. Joseph Leyare* was the builder. The cockpit is completely open and was powered by a 75 hp. *Leighton* engine, which gave her a speed of 21 miles per hour in 1913. The original engine was a 125 hp., 6 cylinder 2 cycle *Brenna*. This was changed to a 125 hp. *Scripps* engine by the 1970's.

THIS 1910 PHOTO SHOWS *GEORGE C. BOLDT* **STANDING IN THE** *P.D.Q.*

With its cedar and brass fittings, the *P.D.Q.* was at one time the fastest boat on the St. Lawrence River and trimmed up everything it came into contact with. *Mr. Boldt's* daughter *Louise Clover,* always piloted this boat during the races and was the first young lady to do such a stunt. She was considered one of the most enthusiastic motor boat women on the river and was always ready and willing to place her boat in a race.

On Saturday, July 28, 1906, the first of the series of races under the auspices of the *St. Lawrence River Yacht Club* were held over a 21 mile course, three times around Whiskey Island, starting and finishing in front of Staples Island. The day and the water were perfect for racing and although there was not a very large crowd to witness them, the races were close and exciting.

The four boats entered the named race were the *P.D.Q.* owned by *George C. Boldt; Roma,* owned by *Louis T. Hunt; Got-To-Go* owned by *William B. Hayden;* and *No Name,* owned by *Mr. Miller* of Clayton, New York. Only two boats finished the race. They were the *P.D.Q.* and the *Roma.* The *P.D.Q.* won the race in 1.02:20 time and *Roma* in second place with 1.03:50 time.

The second race of the day, a free for all, was called at 4:00 pm and was more closely contested and more exciting than the matched race. Five boats entered the free for all. The *P.D.Q.,* owned by *George C. Boldt,* the *So Long II,* owned by *George S. Hasbrouck;* the *Pirate,* owned by *Alexander R. Peacock;* *Got To Go,* owned by *William B. Hayden;* and *No Name,* owned by *Mr. Miller.* Only three out of the five finished the race. They were the *P.D.Q,* the *So Long II,* and the *Pirate.*

The *So Long II* got a much better start than the other boats and kept adding to the gap till the third time around the course when *Pirate* closed in and made the final difference in 28 seconds time. The finish of the race was the most exciting part. The *So Long II,* although winning the race found a better proposition in the form of the *Pirate,* the elapsed time being as follows: *So Long II* 54:10, *Pirate* 54:88, and the *P.D.Q* at 1:04.30. *Pirate* had a 150 horsepower *Trident* engine in her.

Entries for a Saturday motorboat race under the auspices of the *Thousand Islands Yacht Club* on August 4, 1906 were to begin at 2:30 p.m. This was a qualifying race to select which boats were to represent the *Thousand Islands Yacht Club* for the *American Power Boat Association's Gold Cup Challenge Cup.*

The first race entries were: the *P.D.Q.* owned by *George C. Boldt* and driven by *Miss Louise Clover Boldt; So Long II*, owned by *George Hasbrouck; Pirate*, owned by *Alexander R. Peacock;* and *Roma*, owned by *Louis T. Hunt.* The course was three times around Whiskey Island.

The second race of the day was at 3:30 p.m. and was a free for all for boats under 2-horse power and under. This was open to all boats of the St. Lawrence River area. The course was three times around the club burgee off the foot of Lloyd's shoal. The entries were *Tim*, owned by *Lochart Wilbur; Lewella Gorden*, owned by *Gorden C. Kenyon; Tozer*, owned by *George C. Boldt Jr.; Grim*, owned by *Miss S. G. Packer; Bobolink*, owned by *Fred C. Duclon; P.D.S.*, owned by *G. S. Taylor*, and *Margurite*, owned by *Miss Hubbard.*

The thrird race was held at 4:30 p.m. and was a handicap race and was open to members of any recognized yacht club. The course was three times around Whiskey Island, which was 20 and 7/8 miles. Silver cups were awarded to first and second place boats. Entries for this race were: *Breeze*, owned by *G. T. Rafferty; P.D.Q.* owned by *George C. Boldt* and driven by *Miss Louise Clover Boldt; Governor*, owned by *George C. Boldt Jr.; Ina*, owned by *A. T. Hagan, So Long II*, owned by *George Hasbrouck; Lena*, owned by *Stephen Bonsal, Jr.; Pirate*, owned by *Clarence N. Peacock; Joe Gish*, owned by *Ernest Serrell, Sirocco*, owned by *I. P. Wiser; Pixie*, owned by *G. S. Hasbrouck,; and Got To Go*, owned by *William B. Hayden.*

Again more racing with the *P.D.Q.* was held one week later on Saturday August 11, 1906. Hosted under the auspices of the *St. Lawrence River Yacht Club* it was a grand success, and were the best ever held on the river. The day was a perfect one, there not being a ripple on the water, and the whole town turned out to witness the races.

It was the second race of the day that *George C. Boldt's P.D.Q.* was entered. The other boats were the *Got To Go*, owned by *W. B. Hayden*, and the *Eureka*, owned by *J. B. Reid.* The boats were quite evenly matched in regard to speed, but the *Eureka* proved to be the better boat, and won 2 minutes and 22 1/2 seconds ahead of *Got To Go*, and 4 minutes, 46 and 1/2 seconds ahead of the *P.D.Q.*

The *Eureka* was built for *Mr. Reid* that summer for the *Gold Cup Challenge Cup* race that was held at Chippewa Bay in July, but the day before the race she was disabled and unable to enter. *Eureka* was built by *Captain Andrew C. Duclon* of Alexandria Bay, and only had a 20 horse power *Fairbanks* engine, which propelled her an average speed of 23.14 mile over the 21 mile course. *Mr. Hayden's* boat had two 35 horsepower engines and the *P.D.Q.* had a 60 horse power engine.

Several of the boats in the race disqualified themselves by running over their time, so this materially helped the Dixie to win out as she did. The *Got To Go*, owned by *William B. Hayden*; the *P.D.Q.*, owned by *George C. Boldt*; and the *So Long II*, owned by *George S. Hasbrouck*, were disqualified for running ahead of their time. The *Jack* was penalized 2 minutes and 3 seconds, and the *Jewel* was penalized 2 minutes and 39 seconds for starting ahead of time. Following are the summaries of the races:

HANDICAP				FREE FOR ALL - Course 19 1/4 miles		
Name	Start	Finish	Elapsed time	Name	Start	Finish
Ina	4:00	5 25 57	1 25 57	**So Long II**	2:30	3 17 20
Durno	4:00	5 18 46	1 18 46	**Dixie**	2:30	3 11 20
Guess again	4:02	5 13 30	1 11 30			
Jack	4:02	5 15 12	1 15 09			
Roma	4:04	5 22 05	1 17 14			
Jewel	4:05 36	5 12 32	1 09 35			
Got To Go	4:10 59	5 06 32	55 41			
P.D.Q	4 10 51	5 18 19	1 02 28			
So Long II	4 21 21	5 11 52	50 31			
Dixie	4 24 33	5 13 18	48 45			

There were only two boats entered in the free for all, the *Dixie* and *So Long II*. The race was very exciting from the start to finish, although the *So Long II* had the misfortune to break her steering gear, which made her lose some time on turning the buoy. The course was 21 miles, which was three times around Whiskey Island. The boats finished in the following order: *Dixie, Guess Again, Jewel, Jack, Durno, Roma,* and *Ina*.

The *Thousand Islands Yacht Club* held a free for all and a handicap race at Alexandria Bay on Saturday August 25, 1906 and the *Dixie,* owned by *E. J. Schroeder* of the *New York Athletic Yacht Club* won both races.

THOUSAND ISLAND YACHT CLUB ON WELCOME ISLAND – MR. BOLDT WAS VICE – COMMODORE THERE IN 1908.

George C. Boldt was Vice-Commodore of the *Thousand Islands Yacht Club* whose clubhouse was on Welcome Island. He held the position in 1908, and *Gilbert T. Rafferty* was the Commodore. *George C. Boldt Jr.* and his brother-in-law *Alfred Graham Miles* were members also. The *Thousand Islands Yacht Club* was organized in 1894 and incorporated in 1897. Annual dues in 1908 were $50.00.

George C. Boldt Sr. and *Jr.* and *Alfred Graham Miles* were also members of the *Chippewa Yacht Club* at Chippewa Bay, New York in the Thousand Islands and the *P.D.Q.* was listed in their 1912 directory.

Currently the *P.D.Q.* is on loan to the *Thousand Islands Bridge Authority* and is on public display at the *Boldt Yacht House* on Fern Island off Wellesley Island. The *New York State* registration number of the *P.D.Q.* is NY4395 BZ.

The *P.D.Q.* was not listed with the watercraft owned by *Mr. Boldt* on the July 14,1917 inventory of boats. There were others he owned that also were not included in that appraisal. It is assumed that the *P.D.Q.* was sold to *Mr. Edward John Noble* along with much of the *Boldt* properties in 1925. The *P.D.Q.* eventually became the possession of *Mr. Arve S. Wikstrom* of Skaneateles, New York. The *P.D.Q.* was first place winner in the 1969 *Antique Boat Show* hosted by the *Shipyard Museum*. *Mr. Wikstrom's* estate donated the *P.D.Q.* in 1979, to the *Shipyard Museum,* (now known as the *Antique Boat Museum*), Clayton, New York.

THE *P.D.Q.* AMONG OTHER NOTEABLE WOODIES AT THE *ANTIQUE BOAT MUSEUM*

LOUISE CLOVER BOLDT MILES   **and her husband**   **ALFRED GRAHAM MILES**

October 31, 1883 to May 30 1963 – 79 years   **September 5, 1875 to ?**

LOUISE CLOVER BOLDT was a very bright and athletic gal who enjoyed the outdoors and competing at tennis and motor boat racing. She won a number of trophies at the sports she entered into. Her love for the Thousand Island region was as deep as was her parents as she retained *Hopewell Hall* as her summer home when at the St. Lawrence River. This estate was passed on to her and *Alfred Graham Miles's* only daughter, *Clover Wotherspoon Miles* who kept it throughout her lifetime as well.

Louise Clover Boldt was born at 1313 Locust Street in Philadelphia, Pennsylvania on October 31, 1883. She was educated at the *Spence School* in New York City. When she was 16 she was confirmed, along with her mother, on April 8, 1900 at *St. Thomas Church* in New York City. *Clover* lived much in "retirement" on account of her mother's long illness and death on January 7, 1904.

Young *Clover* was a very clever girl and was introduced to society around 1904, after the death of her mother. She became engaged in April of 1907 to *Mr. Alfred Graham Miles* of New York City. They were married on October 8, 1907 at *St. Thomas Church* in New York City. She was 23 and *Alfred* was 32 years old.

ALFRED GRAHAM MILES was a colorful character who became the son-in-law to *George C. Boldt* when he married *Mr. Boldt's* only daughter *Louise Clover*. Motor boat racing became *Alfred Graham Miles'* passion. The *P.D.Q.'s* two through six were not owned by *George C. Boldt,* but by *Alfred Graham Miles.* Both he and his wife, *Louise Clover*, were avid motor boat racing enthusiasts.

Alfred Graham Miles was born on September 5, 1875 in New York City. As an adult *Mr. Miles* stood 5 feet 7 and one-quarter inches tall. In 1893, at age 17, he entered *Cornell University* at Ithaca, New York to study architecture. He took an active interest in athletics and enjoyed sports. Nicknamed *"Gus"* or *"Willie"* he left *Cornell* during his junior year.

Alfred Graham Miles passion for boat racing went beyond driving his own *P.D.Q.* boats. In August 1910 the *Thousand Islands Yacht Club* hosted the international motor boat races along with the *Royal St. Lawrence Yacht Club*. There were eight entries for this race and by the time the boats lined up for the start there were only the *Pioneer, Dixie II, Zigorella* and *Squaw* that showed up, the others for some reason being unable to enter. *Alfred Graham Miles* was the pilot for the *Pioneer*.

The first day the four boats got away well together, the *Pioneer* starting far in the race. On the first leg the *Pioneer* was first, *Dixie II* second *Squaw* third and the *Zigorella* quitting the race at this point. The second leg, the *Pioneer* struck a log or something floating in the river and bent her wheel, which let the *Dixie II* get far in the lead, and when the *Squaw* and *Pioneer* were making the turn at *Ironsides*, the *Squaw* caught fire, the *Pioneer* turning around and going to her assistance. Thus the *Dixie II* finished the race alone making very fast time.

The cause of the *Squaw* catching fire was understood to be from the gasoline pipe breaking off at the same time the engine back fired, setting fire to the escaping gasoline. The boat contained *Mr. George Bourne*, the owner, *Ralph Reid,* who was piloting her, and *Charles Hoffman*, the engineer. *Hoffman* immediately got his fire extinguishers at work but could not put out the fire and *Mr. Alfred Graham Miles*, who was piloting the *Pioneer,* seeing them in trouble, turned about and went back to their assistance.

ALFRED GRAHAM MILES IN HIS *P.D.Q. II* WITH ENGINEER *FRED W. ADAMS*

Just as the *Pioneer* got within a short distance of the burning boat her engines stopped and *Mr. Miles* came to the conclusion that the only way they could be of assistance was to go overboard and swim to them with the fire extinguishers, which he did. These fire extinguishers were used up but the fire was not yet out, and the steam yacht *Irene II*, owned by *Alexander R. Peacock*, was signaled, and came to their assistance, and with a stream of water succeeded in extinguishing the fire, but not until after serious damage had been done to the engine and hull. *Mr. Hoffman* was also quite badly burned about the face and hands. Much credit was due to *Mr. Alfred Graham Miles* for his bravery, also to *Mr. Hoffman* who stuck to the boat until the fire was out. The persons on the *Pioneer* were also entitled to considerable credit inasmuch as they were sure to sacrifice the race when they turned back.

P.D.Q. II,   P.D.Q. III,   P.D.Q. IV,   P.D.Q. V, and   P.D.Q. VI

P.D.Q. II - *Mr. Fred W. Adams* was the person in charge of *George C. Boldt's* flotilla of watercraft. He was born in 1885. Functioning in more than a managerial role, *Adams* was also responsible for the design and construction of *Alfred Graham Miles's* race boats. These perennially competitive and regionally well known watercraft were numbered *PDQ* II through VI. These boats campaigned for about 10 years, ending in 1916.

The peak was reached with the 1912 capture of the *American Power Boat Association's Gold Cup* races. *Alfred Graham Miles* was a challenger in the 3-day event held at the Thousand Islands. From August 1st to the 3rd of 1912 he competed in the international motor boat races that were held over the *Thousand Islands Yacht Club* course on the St. Lawrence River. *Alfred Graham Miles* represented the *Thousand Islands Yacht Club* of Welcome Island, Alexandria Bay, New York.

Alfred was driving the *PDQ II* and *Fred Adams* was the engineer, administering to the well being of the engine. It was powered by a 65 hp. *Sterling* engine that propelled the hard-chined, single-step 26 foot hull at a speed of 45 miles per hour. It had a 6 foot 6 inch beam. The *P.D.Q. II* won the race, which was held on the St. Lawrence River over a 32 statute mile course. The *Gold Cup* offered to the winner was very handsome and made to order at a cost exceeding $800.00. The coveted gold plated urn was marked *Sterling* silver on the bottom.

American Power Boat Association's Gold Cup Challenge Cup Race.
Thousand Islands Yacht Club - August 1, 2, 3, 1912

Boat	Club	Owner
Guess Not	Clayton Yacht Club	H.N. Denny
Wasp	Syracuse Yacht Club	William Tousey
Syracuse	1000 Id. Park Yacht Club	Mrs. C. L. Tousey
Ankle Deep	Lake George R.A.	Count Mankowsk
Bear Cat	Chippewa Yacht Club	H.E. Coppell
Mit II	St. Lawrence River Yacht Club	J. H. Hayden
Baby Reliance	Motor Boat Club of America	J. S. Blackton
P.D.Q II	1000 Island Yacht Club	Alfred Graham Miles

ST. LAWRENCE RACE COURSE - 32 NAUTICAL MILES

Mr. J. B. Reid was the official surveyor of the course for *The American Power Boat Association*.

THE RACE - Start over starting line, three times around, leaving all buoys to port, finishing through starting line thereby covering southwest end of course but twice making actual racing distance 28 "*nautical miles*" and 349 feet, or 33 statute miles and 349 feet.

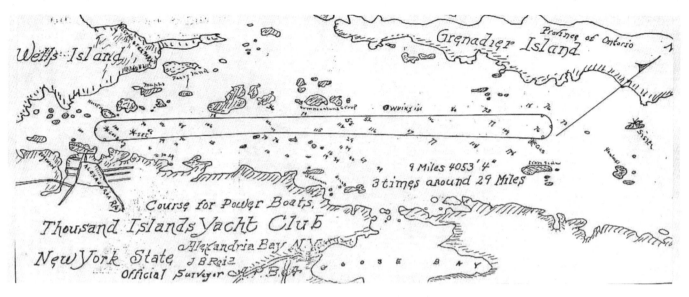

THE *P.D.Q. II* SPEEDING UP THE ST. LAWRENCE RIVER AND FLYING THE *THOUSAND ISLANDS YACHT CLUB* FLAG

The *Wasp* had twin-screws and was powered by 120 hp. *Leighton* engines. Both engines were 6 cylinder with characteristic engine pipes. It represented the *Syracuse Yacht Club*. The race boat *Syracuse* had four 50 hp. *Leighton* engines and had twin screws. It represented the *Thousand Island Park Yacht Club*. The *P.D.Q. II* represented the *Thousand Islands Yacht Club* and had a 65 hp. *Sterling* engine.

START - One gun flying start, with a preparatory gun five minutes before starting time. One red ball will drop one minute after preparatory gun, second in two minutes, third in three minutes, fourth in four minutes, then starting gun end of fifth minute.

The starting gun was fired at 4:30 p.m. and the *Mit II* and *P.D.Q. II* started almost even, followed by *Guess Not*, *Wasp* and *Syracuse*. *Baby Reliance*, although the last one over the line soon took the lead and held it throughout the race. She led *P.D.Q. II* by 27 seconds at the end of the round. *Wasp* was 30 seconds ahead of *Guess Not*, but had engine trouble in the second round and finished the round 1 minute 25 seconds after *Guess not*. Although the course was not very rough, *Syracuse* did not seem able to keep headed in the right direction. She got away from the helmsman twice, doing a *"round turn"* both times. She kept in last place throughout the race. *P.D.Q. II* finished 20 seconds behind *Baby Reliance* and 2 minutes 56 seconds ahead of *Guess Not*, who was followed by *Wasp*, *Mit II* and *Syracuse*. *P.D.Q. II* now had fifteen points to her credit; *Guess Not* and *Baby Reliance* each had thirteen; *Wasp*, eleven; *Mit II*, eight, and *Syracuse* six.

***ALFRED GRAHAM MILES P.D.Q. II* RACING DOWN THE ST. LAWRENCE RIVER AND PAST THE *THOUSAND ISLAND HOUSE* AT ALEXANDRIA BAY, NEW YORK**

During the first day's race *Ankle Deep's* owner and pilot were thrown in the water near Brown's Island and were brought to the judges boat by the *Mit II*. The *Bear Cat* and *Baby Reliance* both developed engine trouble which eliminated them on that day. *Baby Reliance* was owned by *Commodore J. Stuart Blackton* of Brooklyn, New York, which floated the colors of the *Motor Boat Club of America*.

On the third and last day of the series five boats reported for the race, as the *Syracuse* was withdrawn, her owner not wishing to take a chance on her during a *"round turn"* among the other boats in the race. The starting gun was fired at 4:00 p.m. *P.D.Q. II* got off first closely followed by *Guess Not* and *Mit II*, with *Wasp* a little behind them. *Baby Reliance* crossed about 25 second after the gun but she quickly passed the other four boats and took the lead. Their order at the end of the first round was *Baby Reliance*, *P.D.Q. II*, *Wasp*, *Guess Not* and *Mit II*. They all ran consistently and finished in the above order. *Baby Reliance* sprung a leak during the race and finished with a fair cargo of water, but did not seem to have any trouble in maintaining first place.

SUMMARY — First Day - August 1st - Start 4:30 p.m.

BOAT	El Time 1st round M.S.	El Time 2nd round M.S.	El Time 3rd round M.S.	Finish H.M.S	El Time H.M.S	Daily pts.	Total pts.
Guess Not	18:52	18:53	18:55	5:26:40	0:56:40	7	
Wasp	18:35	21:23	18:45	5:28:43	0:58:43	6	
Syracuse	19:46	23:36	at sundown			3	
Ankle Deep	sank at 1st turn						
Bear Cat	18:12	melted out bearings					
Mit II	26:00	23:22	20:50	5:40:12	1:10:12	4	
Baby Reliance	16:42	16:30	29:33	5:32:45	1:02:45	5	
P.D.Q II	17:05	17:34	17:33	5:22:12	0:52:12	8	

Second Day - August 2nd - Start 4 p.m.

BOAT	El Time 1st round M.S.	El Time 2nd round M.S.	El Time 3rd round M.S.	Finish H.M.S	El Time H.M.S	Daily pts.	Total pts.
Guess Not	18:40	18:51	18:46	4:56:17	0:56:17	6	13
Wasp	18:10	20:46	19:30	4:58:26	0:58:26	5	11
Syracuse	24:22	23:12	21:13	5:08:47	1:08:47	3	6
Mit II	20:30	20:52	21:10	5:02:32	1:02:32	4	8
Baby Reliance	16:55	17:53	18:13	4:53:01	0:53:01	8	13
P.D.Q II	17:22	17:48	18:11	4:53:21	0:53:21	7	15

Third Day - August 3rd - Start 4 p.m.

BOAT	El Time 1st round M.S.	El Time 2nd round M.S.	El Time 3rd round M.S.	Finish H.M.S	El Time H.M.S	Daily pts.	Total pts.
Guess Not	19:03	19:10	18:59	4:57:12	0:57:12	5	18
Wasp	18:12	18:10	17:58	4:54:20	0:54:20	6	17
Mit II	20:31	21:00	20:54	5:02:25	1:02:25	4	12
Baby Reliance	17:17	17:46	16:52	4:51:55	0:51:55	8	21
P.D.Q II	17:49	17:46	17:49	4:53:24	0:53:24	7	22

El time 1st round - 2nd round - 3rd round - finish total - El time - Daily points

	1st round	2nd round	3rd round	finish total	El time	Daily points
1st day	17:05	17:34	17:33	5:22:12	0:52:12	8
2nd day	17:22	17:48	18:11	4:53:21	0:53:21	7
3rd day	17:49	17:46	17:49	4:53:24	0:53:24	7

Alfred Graham Miles drove the *P.D.Q. II* to victory. The starting time was at 4:30 pm on August 1st. *Mr. Miles* did the course in 52 minutes and 12 seconds. The next day, August 2nd, the starting time was 4:00 pm and *Mr. Miles* ran 53 minutes 21 seconds in the *P.D.Q. II*. The final day August 3rd the race also started at 4:00 pm and he obtained a time of 53 minutes 24 seconds. There were four other boats in the final race.

P.D.Q. III - *Alfred Graham Miles's* boat *P.D.Q. III* was a product of redesigning by *Charles Duclon* of Alexandria Bay, New York.
    Alfred brought the drawings for the boat from New York City. *Captain Fred Adams, Miles* own boat builder suggested they get *"Charles to see what he can do with the design." Duclon* thought of the boat along *Hacker* lines and it was constructed. The *P.D.Q. III* was entered in the *Gold Cup* race in 1913 and did not win.

The entries for the *Gold Cup* races of the *American Power Boat Association* in 1913 were the *Ankle Deep* of the *Lake George Racing Association*; the *Sand Burr III*, a new challenger from the *Atlantic City Yacht Club*; the *Little Joker*, representing the *Tappen Zee Club*; the *P.D.Q. III*, representing the *Chippewa Yacht Club;* the *Live Wire*, from the *Oak Island Yacht Club;* the *Mutt Jr.* entered by the *Kingston Yacht Club.*

There was much speculation as to the relative merits of the three boats, *Mutt III, P.D.Q. III,* and *Mutt Jr.* While it was generally conceded that none of the local boats could compare with the *Ankle Deep* in speed. Interest was mainly centered in the three boats, which were well known in the area.

An annual regatta at the *Gananoque Yacht Club* was held on Wednesday August 13, 1913 which was a civic holiday for this village. The program embraced a variety of aquatic sports. There were motor boat races, canoe races, sailing races, and swimming contests. Excursions from all points along the St. Lawrence River brought throngs of spectators. One of the most interesting of the events arranged was the sailing canoe race between *Ralph Britton* and *Leo Friede. Friede* and *Britton* raced against each other at New York City for the *International Cup* and the former was victorious.

The motor boat race for speed hydroplanes was held. In some respects this contest had greater interest than the *Gold Cup* races as the entries were more evenly matched. The *Mitt III* was entered by *J. Harold Hayden*, the *P.D.Q. III,* by *Alfred Graham Miles*, the *Mutt* by *John Harry*, the *Guess Not* by *Harry Denny*, and the *Live Wire* by *A. M. Powell.*

In the elimination races for the choice of a defender of the *Gold Challenge Cup* the *Mitt III* had little difficulty in passing the *P.D.Q. III*. In the first day's events of the *Gold Cup* series, the *P.D.Q. III* was ahead of *Hayden's* boat. The *Mitt III* broke down in the second day's race so that each boat had one victory over the other to its credit.

 A week later the *P.D.Q.* III was involved in another race held at Alexandria Bay, New York. At no time letting his hydroplane out to its greatest extent, *Jack Vilas* easily defeated the *P.D.Q. III,* in a race held over the *Thousand Islands Yacht Club* course on a Thursday afternoon. The winner was awarded the *Hydro-aero plane Cup* presented by *Commodore Thomas A. Gillespie.*

The first lap finished with the *P.D.Q. III* far in the rear, but according to the rules of the contest, *Vilas* had to volplane with dead motor to the water and exchange passengers. He had been carrying *C. Leavert Hayden* and then took in *Billy Vilas*. The time consumed in this operation allowed the *P.D.Q. III* to pass the aero plane. However, *Vilas* soon overtook and hovered over the motor boat until the last quarter mile when he readily finished some distance ahead.

P.D.Q. IV - Announcement was made in mid-March of 1914 that *Captain Fred Adams*, designer and builder of *Alfred Graham Miles'* hydroplane racing boats had just completed a new 22 foot one step hull with a 6 feet 6 inch beam. A 150-180 horse power special racing *Sterling* engine would be installed and it was expected that it would have a speed of about 46 miles per hour. The hull was very pretty in design and was finished in mahogany with canvas decks, which were painted in white enamel.

SHOWN HERE IS THE *P.D.Q. IV* IN THE *"HANGERS"* AT THE *GEORGE C. BOLDT YACHT HOUSE*, ALEXANDRIA BAY, NEW YORK. NOTE THE OTHER *P.D.Q.'S* INCLUDING THE ONE HUNG ON THE BACK WALL OF THE YACHT HOUSE

Captain Adams had been the designer of the *Miles'* fleet for the past few years and was the rebuilder of the *Dixie Jr.* that won the *Gold Challenge Cup*. In rebuilding that hull he gained several miles of speed and this boat would have several later improvements.

By the end of April of 1914 *Alfred Graham Miles* was at the St. Lawrence River to try out his new speed boat which was launched and made a trial trip. Although the engine was new it made better than 40 m.p.h. He also had another speed boat under construction and it was a question which one would represent the *Thousand Islands Yacht Club* in the *Gold Cup Race* to be held at *Lake George, New York*.

One month later, in mid-May of 1914, *Alfred's* new boat was named *P.D.Q. IV* and had another tryout over the *Thousand Islands Yacht Club* course and made better time than it had on any previous run. Its' rate of speed was 47.57 miles per hour. It was expected that it would do better than this.

P.D.Q. V - Another new hull that was being worked on during that time was completed and her engine had not been installed, but it was expected that she would do better then 50 miles per hour as she was a larger boat and would have double the horse power. *Captain Fred Adams* was very pleased with the work and *Mr. Miles* was quite confident that the *Gold Cup* would be returned to the Thousand Islands again. The *P.D.Q. V* was built by *Captain Fred Adams* for *Alfred Graham Miles*.

THE *P. D. Q. IV* IN THE *THOUSAND ISLANDS YACHT CLUB* BALLROOM ON WELCOME ISLAND

When the *P.D.Q. V* was constructed in 1914, *Alfred Graham Miles* commented that, *"We have made a mile with the boat at the rate of 51 and I have hopes of bettering the speed. The races at Lake George (New York) will decide what kind of an outfit we have."*

The races for the *Gold Cup* of the *American Power Boat Association* was held at Lake George, New York in July of 1914. A grand success with some record speed was made during the three-day event. The *Baby Speed Demon* entered by the *Motor Boat Club of America* was the winner and retained the cup. Since the winning club had no club house and the place for the 1915 meeting had not been chosen, it was hoped that the *Motor Boat Club of America* would choose to have the races over the *Thousand Islands Yacht Club* course on the St. Lawrence River.

Unfortunately the *P.D.Q. V* representing the *Thousand Islands Yacht Club* and owned by *Alfred Graham Miles* and the *P.D.Q. IV* entered by *Mrs. Harty* of Kingston, Ontario, Canada, both were forced to retire due to engine trouble. The *P.D.Q. V* showed great speed leading *Ankle Deep*, last years winner, by a long lead before her engine trouble developed.

Always one for a good race, *Alfred* entered the *P.D.Q. V* at a three-day power boat regatta in September of 1914. The event was held on the Niagara River at Buffalo, New York. The thirty-five mile race was for the championship of *American* and the *Blackton Trophy*. The trophy was given to the *P.D.Q. V* despite the fact that the *Baby Speed Demon II*, owned by *Mrs. Paula H. Blackton* of Brooklyn, finished first. The *American* speed record was broken by *Mrs. Blackton's* speeder, which made the last five miles of the contest in 5:36 minutes at a rate of 53.73 miles per hour. *Commodore Blackton* declined to accept the trophy donated by himself.

ABOVE IS THE *P.D.Q. V* **WIDE OPEN.** *MR. THOMAS A. GILLESPIE* **IS DRIVING AND** *MR. FRED ADAMS* **IS AT THE CLUTCH**

The race started on schedule with six entries. A race horse start was given the boats and all got over the line together. The *Baby Speed Demon II* took the lead and held it throughout the race. The *Buffalo Enquirer* was forced out of the race by engine trouble after going nine miles. The *Baby Reliance* also broke down on the second lap, her engine having burst a valve. *Neptune II* owned by *Lawrence Buhl* of Detroit, Michigan, finished third. The *Kitty Hawk VI* owned by *H. H. Timken* of Detroit, Michigan, experienced engine trouble and was unable to finish the contest.

The summary: *Baby Speed Demon II, Mrs. Paula Blackton,* Brooklyn, first: time 41.48; average speed 50 miles per hour. *P.D.Q. V, Alfred Graham Miles*, Alexandria Bay, New York, second; time 46.60; average speed 45 miles per hour. *Neptune II, Lawrence Buhl,* Detroit, Michigan, third; time, 51.58; average speed, 39.56 miles per hour.

Back at the Thousand Islands *Alfred Graham Miles* made a record run to *Brockville, Ontario, Canada* in late September of 1914. The distance is 24 miles and the time from the *George C. Boldt* yacht house to the Brockville dock was 27 minutes and 10 seconds. This was the fastest any motor boat had ever run on the St. Lawrence River. *Mr. Miles* made the run in the *P.D.Q. V.*

Alfred's P.D.Q. IV motor boat was driven by his wife. *Louise Clover Boldt Miles* raced the *P.D.Q. IV* against the *P.D.Q. V*, which was driven by her husband, and she won. Her speed was recorded as 47 miles per hour, which was the fastest motorboat time ever made by a woman.

THE *P.D.Q. VI* RACING HYDROPLANE HEADING DOWN RIVER WITH THE VILLAGE OF ALEXANDRIA BAY, NEW YORK IN THE BACKGROUND

SHOWN HERE IS THE *P.D.Q. VI* AS IT ENTERS THE *BOLDT YACHT HOUSE*. THE STEAM TUG *QUEEN* THAT *MR. GEORGE C. BOLDT* OWNED IS IN THE BACKGROUND

In an October 25, 1914 article by *William Washburn Nutting,* he writes, *"In P.D.Q. Fred Adams has produced a finished boat in every particular. She is neat and clean as a new pin and has little of the usual appearance of the racing machine. Her freeboard is high all around, even at the stern, and her motor does not extend above the deck. She will do about 53 miles per hour on the straightaway, and she travels practically without jumping, indicating just the right placing of the planes and distribution of the weight. Her forward deck is an unbroken stretch of white enamel, and, after she once gets going and settled down to her pace, if it were not for the wind, I believe you could dance a fox-trot on it without much danger of going overboard.."*

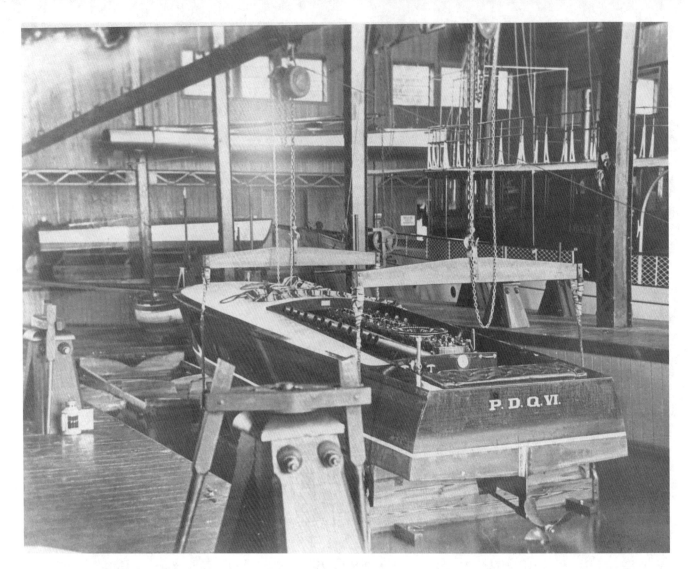

THE *P.D.Q. VI* IN THE *"HANGERS"* INSIDE THE SERVICE BAYS OF THE *BOLDT YACHT HOUSE.* THERE IS A MECHANICAL SYSTEM INCLUDING OVERHEAD CRANE ON DUAL TRACKS, SCREW JACKS FOR RAISING THE VESSELS OUT OF THE WATER FOR SERVICE, AND A STEEL EXPANSION EXHAUST SLEEVE TO THE CUPOLA TO FACILITATE INTERIOR OPERATION OF THE STEAM YACHTS AND GASOLINE ENGINES OF *GEORGE C. BOLDT'S* FLEET OF VESSELS

ONE OF THE *P.D.Q* BOATS OWNED BY *ALFRED GRAHAM MILES* AS IT SPEEDS PAST *BOLDT CASTLE*. BOTH HE AND *LOUISE CLOVER* COMPETED IN MOTOR BOAT RACING.

P.D.Q. VI – was built in the summer of 1915 and was designed in the previous winter by *Captain Fred Adams* and *Alfred Graham Miles*. The P.D.Q. VI measured 24 feet overall and had a 7 foot beam. It was equipped with a 300 horse power *Van Blerck* engine. The boat was completed by August 14, 1915 in time to race at Manhassett Bay for the *Gold Challenge Cup* races. The *P.D.Q. VI* was unable to compete because the aft cylinder in her engine gave out during a trial run. This was the last of the *P.D.Q.'s* to be built and raced until 1920 when she finally retired. Another report said that the *P.D.Q. VI* was powered by a 12 cylinder *Liberty* motor.

It was announced in July of 1917 that the *Thousand Islands Yacht Club Championship Challenge Cup Motor Boat Races* would be held on August 8th 9th and 10th and promised to be of unusual interest. *Mr. Alfred Graham Miles* was chairman of the regatta committee comprised of *Charles M. Englis, George S. Hasbrouck, Houston Barnard, Stephen Bonsal Jr., Chester R. Hoag, William H. Downey, John Englis II, F. B. Lovejoy, James H. Hammond, Lawrence H. Vilas, Marion McMillian, I. H. Jenney* and *Grant Peacock*. These races were an *American Power Boat Association* event. The cup was a beautiful one and cost $1,000.00, the title of which is perpetually to remain in the *Thousand Islands Yacht Club*. In case the cup would be lost to a foreign entrant the winner was allowed to keep it until 30 days prior to the racing event of the following season, when it was to be returned to the *Thousand Islands Yacht Club*. The agreement was that the race is always to be run over the Whiskey Island course.

It is believed that by the 1920's some of the *P.D.Q's* that *Alfred Graham Miles* owned were shipped to New York City. *Mr. Miles* lived at 550 Park Avenue with his wife *Louise Clover* and their daughter *Clover*, when they were not at their Alexandria Bay, New York summer home on Wellesley Island, which was called *Hopewell Hall*.

It was, however, in the summer of 1926 that the *P.D.Q. IV* was in another race. The story goes that several thousand people and hundreds of cars thronged the village of Alexandria Bay, New York on one Monday afternoon during the boat races held under the auspices of the *Sportsman's Association* and the *Chamber of Commerce*. This race program was the first of the summer weekend entertainment planned by the Chamber.

ONE OF THE *P.D.Q.'S* GOING THROUGH ITS PACES. THE *THOUSAND ISLAND HOUSE* AT ALEXANDRIA BAY, NEW YORK IS IN THE BACKGROUND

The first race between boats equipped with *Chevrolet* and marine motors had ten entries. On the first lap the race developed into a contest between three boats with the others running a race of their own half a lap behind. *Jared Massey* came in an easy first with the *Miss Flapper* second and *Eugene Yet* of Watertown, New York third. A purse of $25.00, $15.00, and $10.00 was offered for this race.

The second race entered only boats making about forty miles an hour and not over fifty miles. The boats got off to a good start and ran an even race to the finish. The *Wild Goose* recently purchased by *O. M. Brettenbach* of New York City was winner of first place, the *Duke II* entered by *C. A. Duke* a close second, and the *P.D.Q. IV* owned by *Edward J. Noble* third. The *Chuckle* owned by *W. Charles Lipe* came in fourth.

The third race for boats capable of attaining a speed of fifty miles an hour or better created considerable interest because of the *Baby Gar* boat entered by *Edward J. Noble* of New York City and Alexandria Bay. This type of boat recently raced the *Twentieth Century Limited* down the Hudson River. From the start the *Running Wild* owned by *M. J. Shaughnessy* of Watertown took the lead. On the second lap she looked like a possible winner because she had increased her lead on the *Snail* owned by *Edward J. Noble*. It was on the last lap that the *Snail* was let out and entered the home stretch neck and neck with the *Running Wild*, finally pulling in a length and a half ahead. *Snail* received first place, *Running Wild* second, and the *Wild Goose* third. The *Wild Goose* entered this race to make a race as there were but two entries at the judge's scow when time to call the race.

ABOVE IS ONE OF THE *P.D.Q.'S* GOING THROUGH ITS PACES.

Interest became so keen before the end of the first race that wagers were offered. This interest on the part of the crowd continued throughout all the races. Many of the large crowds were freely expressing pleasure over the races and the manner in which they were conducted. The fact that the races started on the scheduled time appealed to all. Without a doubt races of this type would draw many large crowds to Alexandria Bay.

EDWARD J. NOBLE'S **33 FOOT RUNABOUT NAMED** *SNAIL* **WAS BUILT BY** *GAR WOOD* **IN 1927**

THIS IS BELIEVED TO BE THE 48 FOOT BOAT *PILGRIM* WHICH WAS BURNED AT THE *PEACOCK YACHT HOUSE*. THE *BOLDT YACHT HOUSE* CAN BE SEEN IN THE BACKGROUND

SNAIL was a 33-foot runabout built by *Gar Wood, Inc.* in 1927 and was powered by a 12 cylinder, 450 horse powered *Packard Liberty* engine. *Snail* was owned by *Edward J. Noble* who had bought almost all the *George C. Boldt* estate at the Thousand Islands. This ownership included the *Boldt Yacht House,* which sometimes would be referred to as the *Noble Yacht House*. The *Snail* would eventually become the property of *Mr. Howard F. Miller* of Vergennes, Vermont. It was refurbished in 1985-1986 by *Turcotte Bros.* of Cohoes, New York.

PILGRIM – was a 48-foot maghony boat owned by *Louise Clover Boldt* and believed to be burned at *Peacock Yacht House.*

PRESTO – was a steam yacht designed by *Charles Dell Mosher* of New York City, and built in 1897 by *S. Ayers & Sons* of Nyack, New York. The power plant was a quadruple expansion engine that was listed as two 4 cylinders, 6, 9, 12 & 16 X 8 *Mosher* 1 b engine. The engine was built at the *W. T. Zell & Mosher* plant in Pamoby, New Jersey. Construction was composition. It had a trunk cabin and registration number was 150764. Net tons were 15 with gross tons at 22. Overall length was 80 feet 4 inches. At the waterline it was 75 feet. The beam was 9 feet 6 inches and the depth was 4 feet 2 inches, which gave the *Presto* a draft of 3 feet. Its speed was 30 miles per hour.

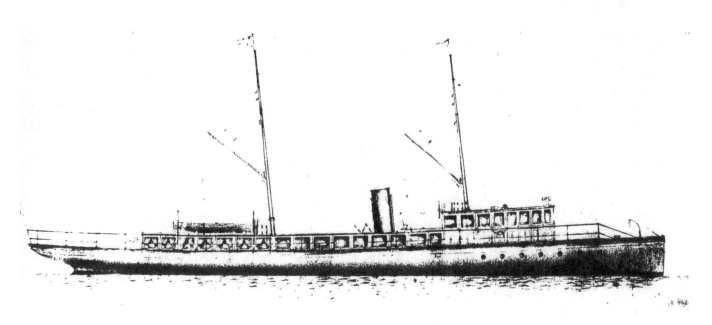

GEORGE C. BOLDT'S **80 FOOT STEAM YACHT** *PRESTO*

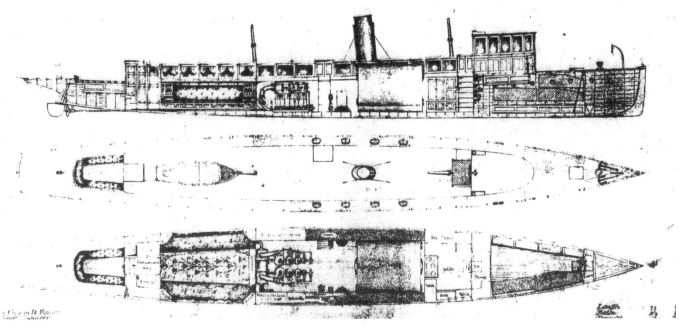

THE *PRESTO* INSIDE THE *BOLDT YACHT HOUSE* ON FERN ISLAND. THE DESIGNER OF THE *PRESTO* WAS *CHARLES DELL MOSHER* OF NEW YORK CITY WHO CAME TO INSPECT THE STEAM YACHT IN AUGUST 1903. THIS FAST BOAT WAS OWNED BY *GEORGE C. BOLDT* AND AFTER SOME SPEEDY TRIALS THE BOAT WAS TAKEN TO OGDENSBURG, NEW YORK FOR A NEW BOILER.

It is uncertain when *George C. Boldt* obtained the *Presto* and from whom. His use of this boat must have been short because records indicate that it was owned by *Mr. John W. Sullivan* of New York City during 1907 and in 1908 he had the steam engine removed. Port of registry and home port was New York, New York. In 1910 the *Presto* became the property of *H. A. Smythe Martin*. The home port and port of registry remained New York, New York.

GEORGE C. BOLDT'S **80 FOOT STEAM YACHT** *PRESTO*

QUEEN - The steam tug *Queen* was built in Buffalo, New York in 1897 by *J. B. Souter.* Hull construction was of steel. The registration number was 20616 and weight was 29 tons net. The *Queen* was 50 feet 7 inches long and had a 14-foot beam with a depth of 6 feet 2 inches. Three years later *George C. Boldt* purchased the *Queen* from its builder for $4,900.00 on November 22, 1900.

There are two courses the steam tug *Queen* could have used to get to the Thousand Islands. The most likely and more practical way would be through the *Erie Barge Canal* heading east to the Oswego River and Oswego Canal heading north to Lake Ontario. From there the course would turn northeasterly to the St. Lawrence River to its' new home at Alexandria Bay, New York.

The other course from Buffalo, New York where the *Queen* was purchased, to the Thousand Islands, would be to head out the *Erie Marina Basin* and go across Lake Erie to the Welland Canal in Ontario, Canada. Heading north through the canal to Lake Ontario, the steam tug *Queen* then would cross the lake in a northeasterly direction to the St. Lawrence River and on to the *Boldt* estate at Wellesley Island, Alexandria Bay, New York.

Regardless of which course the *Queen* took to get to the Thousand Islands, the fact is that it was there that it found a new home at the *Boldt Yacht House* to serve the many and varied uses for *George C. Boldt* and his staff of employees.

THE 50 FOOT 7 INCH STEEL HULLED STEAM TUG *QUEEN* WAS *GEORGE C. BOLDT'S* "WORK HORSE" AT HIS THOUSAND ISLAND ESTATE. IN THE BACKGROUND ON THE LEFT IS *HEART ISLAND*. *IMPERIAL ISLAND* IS ON THE RIGHT

The steam tug *Queen* proved to be the *"work horse"* for *George C. Boldt*'s many projects and may not have sat idle for the following 16 years he owned it. By the November 22, 1900 date he purchased it, work was well underway clearing the site on *Heart Island* for his new summer home which would become known as *Boldt Castle*. By August of that year, three steam drills were employed in blasting rock to a depth of 10 feet for the foundation. *Mr. J. B. Reid*, a contractor from Alexandria Bay, New York and 150 workmen carried on the job. The work on the house was not to be rushed. It was expected that it would take at least three years to build it.

The *Queen* was used for towing scows of stone from Oak Island to *Heart Island* for the building of *Boldt Castle*. Barge after barge of stone would make the 10 mile one way trip up the St. Lawrence River from the Oak Island quarry. Certainly there would have been a lot of rubble on *Heart Island* after the wood frame cottage was removed to make room for the new summer home. In addition to all the debris left from the newly built *Alster Tower, Arch of Honor, Peristyle*, and the *Power House – Clock Tower* besides the six summerhouses, built of rustic stone. All this before *Mr. Boldt* bought the steam tug *Queen*.

Legend has it that *George C. Boldt* went out on the frozen river and drew a circle on the ice for an island to be built on that spot. It was said that all the debris from the *Heart Island* work was dumped here for the *"creation"* of this island which is known as Belle Island, on which he would eventually build a beautiful *Dutch Colonial* house and sell to *Alexander R. Peacock*.

THIS PHOTOGRAPH WAS TAKEN ON APRIL 13, 1912 AT ALEXANDRIA BAY, NEW YORK. DRIFT ICE SURROUNDS THE TUG *QUEEN* WHICH WAS QUITE LATE FOR ICE TO STILL BE IN THE ST. LAWRENCE RIVER.

In addition, the *Queen* was used for towing scows loaded with produce from the *Boldt* farm on Wellesley Island to the mainland, (most likely to Clayton, New York), where they would then be shipped to *Mr. Boldt's* hotels in New York City and Philadelphia, Pennsylvania. Called *Wellesley Island Farms,* this highly productive and modern operation was most likely Mr. Boldt's *"pet project,"* for being a gentlemen farmer seemed to be his greatest love.

As you have read *George C. Boldt's* houseboat, the *LaDuchesse* was also towed from place to place by the steam tug *Queen.* This powerful vessel kept the captain and crew busy. Work for them must have not only been challenging but also rewarding to ply the waters of the beautiful St. Lawrence River in the pristine area of the Thousand Islands.

THE STEAM TUG *QUEEN* CUTTING THROUGH THE ICE COVERED ST. LAWRENCE. *IMPERIAL ISLAND* IS IN THE BACKGROUND. BELOW ARE UNIDENTIFIED PEOPLE IN FRONT OF THE STEAM TUG *QUEEN* AT ALEXANDRIA BAY, NEW YORK

A *"SALVAGE OPERATION"* AT THE CORNWALL DOCK, ALEXANDRIA BAY. THE LARGE SCOW WITH ITS' *"A FRAME"* DERRICK COULD HAVE BEEN OWNED BY *GEORGE C. BOLDT* AND ONCE USED FOR THE BUILDING OF *BOLDT CASTLE*. THE TUG BOAT TO THE LEFT LOOKS LIKE THE *QUEEN* WHICH *MR. BOLDT* OWNED. ADDITIONAL RESEARCH WILL BE DONE TO CORRECTLY IDENTIFY THESE VESSELS

It was on a Saturday in May of 1904 that the steamer *Riverside* was launched from the *Thurston's Shipyard* on Walton Street at the lower bay in Alexandria Bay, New York. The steam tug *Queen* towed it to the *Dana* dock to have a new engine installed in it.

But not all the duties for the steam tug *Queen* were interesting, exciting, or challenging. Some were very unexpected and tragic. An early morning fire hit one Friday at the *Thousand Island Park* on Wellesley Island in early May of 1904. Nine summer cottages, entailing a loss of about $20,000.00 were lost in the blaze. The fire broke out about 10:00 a.m. and assistance from Alexandria Bay and Clayton, New York was summoned.

**THE STEAM TUG *QUEEN* AT THE *BOLDT YACHT HOUSE* WITH THE STEAM YACHT *LOUISE*
IN THE CENTER BAY**

In response to a call for help, the Alexandria Bay fire engine and hose carts were quickly loaded on board *Boldt's* scow *Ark,* and towed by his steam tug *Queen,* started up the St. Lawrence River with about 30 firemen. At 1:00 p.m. the fire was under control.

Without the assistance of the Alexandria Bay and Clayton firemen many more cottages would have been destroyed, as the facilities for fighting fire in the *Thousand Island Park* were limited. The cottages destroyed were at the rear of *The Columbian Hotel.* None of the cottage contents were saved, and no one was reported to have been injured. The cause of the fire was from a man who was raking up leaves and cleaning lawns setting fire to a pile of leaves, and soon the fire spread through the dry grass and beneath the cottage of *Dr. Bailey,* who was from Adams Center, New York. His cottage soon caught on fire, then spread to the adjoining cottages.

The *Queen* underwent extensive repairs at the *Thurston Shipyard* on Walton Street in Alexandria Bay, New York during the winter of 1910-1911. By April 1911 it was launched and taken to Clayton, New York where a new boiler was installed. By May the work was complete and the *Queen* was again in commission.

During a disastrous fire in August of 1911 at the *Frontenac Hotel* on Round Island, *Mr. George C. Boldt* ordered the crew of the *Queen* to the scene, to assist in saving and carrying away property and passengers.

The *Queen* was operated by *Captain Zoller* who did not lay her up for the winter of 1912 – 1913 until February 6, 1913, at which time she made her last trip across the St. Lawrence River and at that same time people were crossing on foot a few hundred feet below. By the end of March of that year she was fitted out and began running again. The steam tug *Queen* was used for trips to Clayton and Ogdensburg, New York all winter for materials.

THE STEEL HULLED TUG *QUEEN* WAS RENAMED THE *CARLOTTA* AND IS SEEN HERE
IN THE BUFALO, NEW YORK HARBOR

In late January of 1914, the St. Lawrence River was not frozen over opposite Alexandria Bay, New York and the tug *Queen* was still making her trips between Alexandria Bay and *Mr. Boldt's Wellesley Island Farm*.

The steam tug *Queen* would leave the Thousand Islands and make its journey back to Buffalo, New York where it was built in 1897. *George C. Boldt* sold the *Queen* on October 21, 1916 to *Mr. Benjamin L. Cowles, President* of *Cowles Towing Company, Inc.,* 360 Ohio Street, Buffalo, New York. *Mr. Cowles* renamed the *Queen* and called it *Carlotta*. He kept the tug from that date until 1929 with the exception of the year 1925 when it was registered by *The United States Railroad Administration* in Buffalo, New York.

According to *Mr. Richard Garrity,* who was in his 80's and lived in Tonawanda, New York, and worked for *Benjamin L. Cowles,* he stated that the tug probably had a 75 hp. steam engine and had a lot of brass. He replaced the engine in 1926 for *Mr. Cowles*, with a 100 hp. *Fairbanks* semi-diesel. He also stated the hull was 1/4-inch steel. The purchase of the steam tug *Queen* gave *Mr. Cowles* a fleet of six steel and four wooden tugs, all of which were stationed in Buffalo, New York. His business was to do harbor towing in the Buffalo area. The *Queen/Carlotta* would also be used in the building and repair of bridges over the *Erie Barge Canal*.

Ownership of the *Queen/Carlotta* transferred in 1938 to *Mr. Clarton P. O'Conner* and *Mr. Wesley H. Ormerod*, both men from Buffalo, New York. *Mr. O'Conner* was a lawyer with an office at 833 Ellicott Square and a residence at 387 Plymouth Avenue. By April 1940 the tug changed hands again, this time to *Mr. Joseph C. Klas*.

The tug *Queen/Carlotta* left the Buffalo area for Philadelphia, Pennsylvania to its new owners, *Mr. Clarence L. O'Conner* and *Mary Kane,* by September of 1943. There the vessel changed ownership in the same year to *Margaret Brooks Branigan* and *Rocheile Brooks*, then soon transferred to *Helen R. Steel* of 550 Rancocas Avenue, Delanco, New Jersey. Philadelphia was listed as homeport.

Louise D. Steel was listed as master of the tug in 1944. In June of 1947, *Mr. Leslie E. Cropper* became master and owner. Three years later, in 1950, ownership reverted back to *Helen R. Steel*. She had a different engine installed, which was a *Buda Engine* built by the *Buda Engine Company* of Harvey, Illinois in 1945. This oil-fueled engine was listed as having 265 horsepower. It was installed on December 5, 1949.

By 1952 the *American Bridge Company* became the owner of the *Queen/Carlotta* with *Mr. Howard G. Whitpan* as master of the tug. *Mr. George G. Wehr* became owner later in 1952. He was listed as being with the *Interstate Terminal & Transportation Company* which was located at Pier 17, North Wharves, Philadelphia, Pennsylvania. Located at the same address was the next title holder to the *Queen/Carlotta*, which was the *Philadelphia Derrick and Salvage Corporation*. They took title in 1956 and by 1962 the *Kent Concrete Company* had possession of the vessel. Cambridge, Maryland became the homeport.

Mr. Robert Bave became the master and owner of the *Queen/Carlotta* in January 1962. He was the president of *Marine Services*, Inc., and his residence was 1205 Ormond Avenue, Drexel Hill, Pennsylvania. Philadelphia again became the homeport for the tug. *Mr. Bave* kept the vessel registered until 1974.

During the summer of 1989 this author went to Drexel Hill, Pennsylvania in search of the *Queen/Carlotta* and its owner. A note of inquiry was left by this author at the Ormond Street address as no one was there. A few weeks later that note was returned with the name and address of where the tug was. I had been in the hospital recovering from major back surgery when my wife brought in the mail. Needless to say, having found the *Queen* aided in my long and difficult recovery!

The owner was *Mr. David R. Stith* of *Underwater Technics, Inc.*, of Camden, New Jersey. He had found it sunk in the Delaware River and had it raised. It was then towed to his business site where vandals would sink it again. *Mr. Stith* had it raised again and beached it on land, and had the engine removed with the intentions of scrapping the tug.

THE STEEL HULLED TUG *QUEEN/CARLOTTA* WAITS SILENTLY FOR ITS FATE AS IT SITS ON THE DELAWARE RIVER IN NEW JERSEY

THE STEEL HULLED *QUEEN/CARLOTTA* ON THE DELAWARE RIVER AT CAMDEN, NEW JERSEY

AND THE FINAL BLOW TO A VERY HISTORIC VESSEL

Thus began a four year long effort by this author to *"Save the Queen"* from destruction. *Mr. Stith* was willing to donate this much used tugboat to a non-profit organization. A number of such organizations were contacted and a few people showed interest in the project. Efforts were underway to try and bring this historical vessel back to the Thousand Islands or to Buffalo, New York where it was built. Unfortunately none were successful and the tug *Queen* was scrapped. *Mr. Stith* had saved the portholes, which are now in this author's possession. One has been restored and adorns my study.

SCOUT * - The motor boat *Scout* was built in 1912 at a length of 36 feet and had a 6 foot 4 inch beam. Its' hull construction was wood and was powered by a gasoline engine. It was appraised on July 14, 1917 for $1,000.00.

SENIOR * - *Mr. Fred Adams* was in charge of all the motor boats owned by *George C. Boldt.* He was a thorough motor boatman and understood every detail of their construction. During the winter of 1912-1913, *Mr. Adams* built for *Mr. Boldt* the pleasure semi-cruiser *Senior.* The hull was 45 feet over all and had a 8 foot 6 inch beam, planked with 3/4 inch selected cork pine, and finished throughout with mahogany. A canopy top or shade deck covers the entire cockpit and has a cabin aft with toilet, etc., and back of the cabin an after cockpit with large upholstered seat. It had two watertight compartments. It was fitted throughout with electric lights and a storage outfit for storing its own storage batteries when the engine is running. The *Senior* was equipped with a 90 hp. *Trebert* engine and had a speed of 18 miles per hour. She was one of the most completely fitted motor boats on the St. Lawrence River and was used by *Mr. Boldt* as his private motor boat. *Mr. Adams* designed and superintended the building of this boat and did so at the request of *Mr. Boldt* who made no suggestions to him, only told him to build a motor boat for his own pleasure.

GEORGE C. BOLDT'S MOTOR BOAT *SENIOR* HEADING TOWARDS THE *BOLDT YACHT HOUSE. BOLDT CASTLE* ON *HEART ISLAND* IS IN THE BACKGROUND

The widowed *Mr. Boldt* was 62 years old in 1913 when the *Senior* was completed. He had worked hard and long for over 45 years. The fruit of his labor was indeed extensive! He had achieved worldwide recognition and fame and as such he remained a very humble individual. So deservedly the 45 foot *Senior* motor boat was *"for his own pleasure"* and what better place in the whole wide world to enjoy it more then in the Thousand Islands.

George C. Boldt was born on the *Island of Rugen* in the Baltic Sea and retained much of his learning from his parents. This training lasted him throughout his lifetime. Interesting that he chose the Thousand Islands to live, and when the end of his life came, it was on the island of Manhattan where he died. Thus he was born on an island, lived on an island, and died on an island.

The *Senior* was appraised by *Mr. James H. Hutchinson* on July 14, 1917 for $3,600.00.

GEORGE C. BOLDT'S** 45 FOOT MOTOR BOAT **SENIOR

SKOL – was built by *Fitzgerald & Lee* at a cost of around $12,000.00 during the winter of 1939. As a triple cockpit runabout it was 31 feet 6 inches long. *Skol* was commissioned by longtime Thousand Islands summer resident *Nils R. Johaneson.* He was the husband of *Clover Wotherspoon Miles,* granddaughter of *George C. Boldt.* The *Skol* was powered by a 300-hp *Scripps* V-12, and was reported to be capable of more than 50 mph. *Hacker* specifies a single piece 2 inch by 3 inch oak keel, 7/8 inch white elm frames on 1 inch centers, and 9/16 inch *Honduras* mahogany planking. The interior abounded in lush touches, even an icebox, and numerous pockets and lockers. A hatch covered the aft cockpit or "rumble seat," as *Hacker* aptly named it, considering the proximity of the *Scripps* V12.

SNOW QUEEN - was an electric launch run by storage batteries and was 20 feet long over all and had a 5 foot beam. Her speed was about 6 miles per hour.

SOPHIA -The steam yacht *Sophia* was built at Alexandria Bay, New York during the winter of 1893-94 for *Captain Harmonius Wellington Visger* by *Mr. Andrew Duclon,* also of Alexandria Bay. The *Sophia* was 75 feet long and had a 11 foot beam. It was powered by a 40 horse power engine. To her waterline she was built of oak; Georgia Pine, above. Her cabin was cherry and contained four berths. Aft of the pilothouse was the galley. In the forecastle where sleeping accommodations for a crew of six. Her speed was 13 miles per hour.

It was in July1894 that *George C. Boldt,* along with *Mr. A. S. L. Shields,* a well-known criminal lawyer from Philadelphia, Pennsylvania, leased the steam yacht *Sophia.* During a two-day fishing trip they caught 400 bass, which were put on display at the *Thousand Island House* where they were staying. Use of the boat *Sophia* enabled Mr. Boldt, his wife Louise, and their children greater access to explore the beauty of the St. Lawrence River and it's many gem-like islands.

THE STEAM YACHT *SOPHIA* WAS PILOTED BY *CAPTAIN HARMONIUS WELLINGTON VISGER* WHO APPEARS IN THE INSERT. *GEORGE C. BOLDT* LEASED THE VESSEL IN JULY 1894. BELOW *SOPHIA* IS THE LARGE VESSEL ON THE LEFT OF BOTH PICTURES

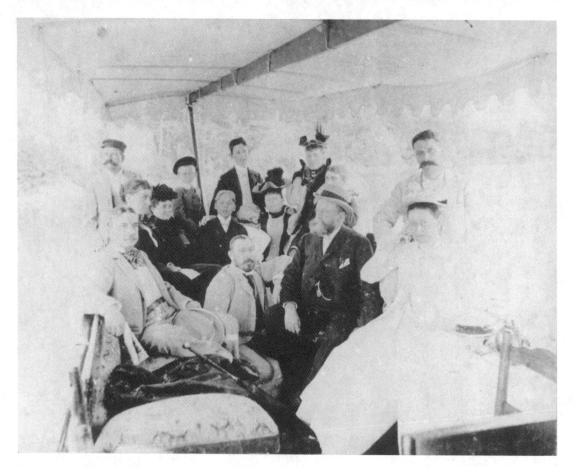

GEORGE C. BOLDT SEATED ON THE FLOOR IN THE CENTER ABOARD THE STEAM YACHT *SOPHIA* WHICH HE RENTED IN JULY 1894. OTHER PASSENGERS ARE UNIDENTIFIED

SQUAB * - By the spring of 1914, *Mr. George C. Boldt* was having a new fire tug built at his yacht house on Fern Island. This boat was called the *Squab* and it was designed by *Captain Fred Adams* and built under his personal supervision. The *Squab* was 38 feet long and had a ten-foot beam. No pains nor expense had been spared to make the *Squab* one of the most useful boats in the *Boldt* fleet. Construction was of wood.

The fire tug *Squab* was used about the *George C. Boldt* estate, which included the many private waterways, and handle lighters, scows, and in case of fire in any of his many cottages or farm buildings.

A 40 horse power *Buffalo* heavy duty engine was installed to propel the *Squab*. In addition, a three-inch *Rumsey* fire dump was attached to the forward end of the motor. A low deckhouse was built over the engine, with a hose reel carrying about 300 feet of hose. The steering wheel and clutch of the engine to the fire pump was on the deck so that it could be controlled by the captain. Besides using as a fire tug, the *Squab* was used to haul scows and do other similar work on the water around the *George C. Boldt* estate.

The fire tug *Squab* attended a number of fires in the region and was credited for limiting the damage done. One such fire was at the *Alexandria Bay Creamery* on March 18, 1914. The *Squab* hastened to the scene of the fire and laid a line along *Otter Creek*. The *Alexandria Bay Creamery*, located just outside the limits of Alexandria Bay, New York, was burned to the ground on the Monday morning blaze which caused $8,000.00 in damage. Besides the building, machinery and equipment, 1,500 pounds of butter were destroyed. A large quantity of cheese was saved.

One of the largest losses by fire in several years occurred at Alexandria Bay one Friday in May 1916. At 3:00 in the afternoon the fire department was called out to a fire that had started at the *Thurston's* shipyard on Walton Street, facing the lower bay.

The fire started in the building where about a ton of oakum was stored and where men were spinning the oakum in readiness to be used on the steam boats on the ways, and within a very few minutes an explosion took place in the building sending the fire in all directions and setting everything ablaze. The fire department responded very promptly and within five minutes after the first sound of the bell two streams of water were playing on the building. Other fire companies arrived and within fifteen minutes seven streams were in action. The fire engine was also hooked on to give more pressure and did good work.

The fire department did excellent work and were entitled to great praise for the manner in which they handled the fire under the direction of *Chief DeYoung*, and it is hardly creditable that one residence on the east side of the fire within twenty feet was wholly saved and another on the west side within five feet was partly saved although the *Thurston Block* standing between the two was entirely burned to the ground.

Besides the *Thurston Block* being valued at $6,000.00, there was also burned the steam yacht *Klotawah* which was owned by *Edson Bradley* of Washington, D. C., which originally cost $125,000.00, but at the time was valued at $30,000.00. A total loss of the new steamer under construction for Morristown, New York parties was valued at $10,000.00. *Thurston's* ways and hoisting engine were valued at $3,000.00. Damage to the steamer *Sport* was valued at $1,000.00. A total of $1,500.00 was the listed damage to the *Willard Davis* house and the small damages to the surrounding property.

Mr. Joseph Northup and *Mr. John W. Estes* who conducted a grocery store in the *Thurston Block*, lost stock which was valued at several thousand dollars. *Mr. John M. Comstock Jr.*, who lived in the *Davis* house lost the majority of his furniture and household effects. *Mr. Northup* and *Mr. Estes* were partly insured and *Mr. Comstock* carried no insurance. *Mr. Edward Furness* family practically lost everything except their piano. *Mr. George Thurston* lost all household furnishings as did also the *Ely* family who resided in the *Thurston Block*.

Several hundred dollars worth of carpenter tools were lost by the following: *C. C. Griffin, Henry Griffin, Byron Wilbur, William Snow, W. H. Cook, George Thurston, Earl Davis, William Truesdell*, and *George Crumwell*. It was stated that *Mr. Thurston's* insurance was about $5,500.00 on block and ways, etc., and $4,000.00 on the new boat being built. The steam yacht *Klotawah* was fully insured as was the steam yacht *Sport. Mr. Willard Davis* also carried a small amount of insurance. It was rumored that *Mr. Thurston* would build an office and engine room of cement and use the balance of the property for his ship building business.

During the fire great assistance was rendered by the Boy Scouts, telephone linemen, and others. Also by firemen from *George C. Boldt's Wellesley Island Farm* who accompanied the fire tug *Squab* from the *Boldt* estate. The fire tug *Squab* belonging to *Mr. Boldt* was at once on the scene of the fire and rendered very valuable assistance to the fire department and in reality saved the steamer *Sport*, which was hauled out on the ways. The fire department extended their thanks to all who helped during this tragedy.

The *Squab* was appraised on July 14, 1917 by *Mr. James H. Hutchinson* of Alexandria Bay, New York. He placed a value of $1,500.00 on the tug at that time and stated that the engine was purchased second hand and was made around 1908-09.

ICE BERG   Not in the remembrance of any the older generation had the Ontario Lake ice reached the thickness and volume which came down the St. Lawrence River in mid-May of 1920. Only one tenth of an iceberg appears above the surface so the depth and weight of the ice can be appreciated. Enormous ice berg's from 10 to 15 feet high were grounded in the upper and lower bays of Alexandria Bay, New York, and swayed back and forth with the wind or the movement of the current but could not float.

Several days of strong wind forced the ice back up stream and crowded every little bay with a grinding mass. Crossing the St. Lawrence River in a small boat was impossible, although the ice-breaking tug *Squab* made her way across from the *Boldt* estate each day. Workmen were unable to get to their island jobs and rush work was at a stand still. The breeze from this open air refrigerator was of winter quality and it was with a sigh of relief that the Alexandria Bay residents saw the ice moving down stream before a south wind.

Although the navigation was declared open on April 22, 1920, and the lighthouse lighted, it was not deemed safe to place the buoys until the lake ice was down. The soundness of this decision was very evident, as it would have meant the entire loss of the apparatus if the buoys had been in position.

Bitter complaint was made at Ogdensburg, New York when the steamer *Kendall* grounded on *Sunken Rock* reef one Friday night because the buoy light which belongs on the shoal was not burning. With a channel on either side a hundred feet deep, she picked the particular spot where the going was not good. The situation was not appreciated then as by the time the ice had traveled 30 miles and swept into a broad, clear channel there was not much to look at.

THIS IS BELIEVED TO BE THE STRANDED STEAMER *KENDALL* GROUNDED ON *SUNKEN ROCK REEF* IN APRIL 1920. *BOLDT CASTLE* ON *HEART ISLAND* IS IN THE BACKGROUND. GEORGE C. *BOLDT'S* TUG BOAT *SQUAB* CAME TO ITS AID.

The *Squab* stood by the stranded steamer *Kendall* and when the *Isabel*, with *Captain Hinckley* arrived with wrecking apparatus, the *Kendall* was lightened somewhat of her coal cargo and pulled off without much damage. The *Isabel* took on the buoys the following Sunday afternoon and was engaged in laying them. Oweing to the fact that the water was unusually low for that season of the year little or no damage seemed to have been done to boathouses and other structures along the waterfront of the St. Lawrence River.

THE *SQUAB* WITH TWO UNIDENTIFIED MEN ABOVE

THE *SQUAB* BEHIND A STONE LADEN BARGE. THE PEOPLE ARE UNIDENTIFIED

ABOVE IS THE *SQUAB*. THE MAN TO THE LEFT OF THE PICTURE WAS *MR. ERNEST POOLE*. NOTE THE NEW PILOT HOUSE WHICH WAS ADDED TO THE VESSEL

The *Squab* became part of the *Edward John Noble* estate when *Mr. Noble* purchased the *Boldt* properties. *Mr. Ernest Porter* was at the helm of the *Squab* in 1924. Later the *Squab* became the property of *Mr. Ernest Poole*, who sold it to *Mr. Lawrence Mallory Jr.* The *Squab* was used to haul most of the cement from Clayton, New York to the construction site for the building of the Thousand Islands Bridge in1938. *Mr. Mallory* terminated his use of the *Squab* and it became the property of *Williams Marine Service* of Lansdowne, Ontario, Canada. It was there that the *Squab* met its fate. It was burned in the summer of 1963. The engine at the time was a *Hall-Scott*, which was said to have been installed at *Hutchinson's Boat Works* of Alexandria Bay, New York.

ABOVE THE FIRE TUG *SQUAB* IS ON THE RIGHT. BELOW THE *SQUAB* IS PULLED UP THE RAILS AT *WILLIAMS MARINE SERVICE* IN LANSDOWNE, ONTARIO, CANADA

The fire tug *Squab* designed by *Captain Fred Adams* and built under his personal supervision met its final days at *Williams Marine Service* which is located in Lansdowne, Ontario, Canada. This Thousand Island business is owned and operated by the brothers *Howard* and *David Williams* who took ownership of this much-used vessel. The tug was 38 feet long and had a ten-foot beam and was wood constructed which was in poor shape. Eventually the engine was pulled out of the *Squab* and the hull was burnt. All that was salvaged from this much-used vessel was a spotlight, which was put on another boat.

UNIDENTIFIED MEN AT *WILLIAMS MARINE SERVICE* WHERE THE *SQUAB* WAS BURNED

THE *ONE DESIGN CLASS*   In an effort to increase the interest in motorboat racing, the *Thousand Islands Yacht Club*, of which *George C. Boldt* was a member, decided to inaugurate a series of races for the summer of 1910 and each year thereafter for a period of four years at least. The *One Design Class* of boats were all to be of the same length, same beam, built by the same maker, from the same drawings, and equipped with the same motor. It was proposed to have the boats as nearly alike as possible and to have them cross the starting line at exactly the same weight.

It was proposed to have the boat itself of moderate length and generous beam, designed for a broad range of utility, and that it should in no sense be a racing machine; also to limit the speed to something between eighteen and twenty miles an hour, thus giving a dependable boat always useful on the St. Lawrence River.

The proposed scheme was due to the fact that it was admitted there was a lack of local interest in motorboat races at the time, due to the relative merits of the different entries being so well known to everyone, that the outcome was a foregone conclusion. While under this plan it was hoped that the element of uncertainty would prevail in every race, and it was urged that the outcome would depend entirely upon the skill of the operator and condition of the motor and not at all on the amount of money that an owner was able or willing to spend. It was decided to limit the number of boats constructed to 20, and the scheme was developed so that a successful outcome was assured.

It was proposed to run the races somewhere on the river every Wednesday and Saturday, for cups of moderate value, and to conclude the series during the *Gold Cup* races with a final heat, this heat being for cups of greater value. It was agreed that if the plan would be carried out, it would ensure close and uncertain finishes and develop a rivalry that would renew interest in motorboat racing to an extent heretofore unknown.

DRAWINGS FOR THE *ONE DESIGN CLASS* MOTOR BOATS. *CHARLES DELL MOWER* - NAVAL ARCHITECT - DESIGNED THE CRAFT. HIS ADDRESS WAS 29 BROADWAY, NEW YORK, NEW YORK

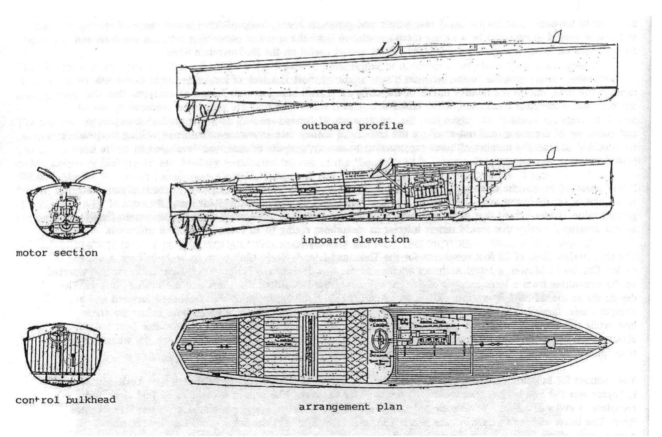

outboard profile

inboard elevation

motor section

control bulkhead

arrangement plan

The *One-Design Class* of 28 foot runabouts for the *Thousand Islands Yacht Club* were to be built from a design by *Mr. Charles D. Mower*, a naval architect whose address was 29 Broadway, New York, New York. He was selected by the committee from a large number of designs submitted by the leading designers and motorboat builders. The design shows a boat 28 feet over all, with 5-foot beam, straight stem with quite high freeboard forward and a straight sheer, carried to the V transom stern. The hull was to have the lines of a speedboat below the water line, while the high freeboard and generous flare of sections would make her dry and comfortable for runabout service. This was achieved by using a displacement hull design, which would cut through the water rather than *"plane"* on the top of it in the fashion of modern race boats.

The contract for building the boats was placed with the *Leyare Boat Works* of Ogdensburg, New York. *Mr. Joseph L. Leyare* was the builder, and twenty boats were built for the class. The equipment was to be first class and complete in every detail and it was expected that the class would prove a very popular one on the St. Lawrence River. The boats were not primarily race boats. They were fast, comfortable family launches, seating six people, built of the finest cedar hulls with oak framing and with deck and trim of fine mahogany.

The engine was a four-cylinder, four-cycle, *Jencick* of 30 h.p. with cylinder 4 and 1/2 by 5 inches installed under flush hatches in the forward deck. A speed of over 18 miles an hour was expected. The cylinders and pistons of semi-steel nickel steel crankshafts, open hearth steel connecting rods, I beam section, with bronze bushings in piston end and *Parsons* white brass in crankshaft end, manganese bronze crank cases with aluminum oil pans, camshafts of one piece of *Krupp* chrome nickel, steel, mounted on Hess-*Bright* bearings, piston pins and push rod parts, all of *Krupp* chrome nickel steel, hardened and ground; minor bearings, such as pump, magneto gears, timing gear, etc., to be mounted on *Hess-Bright* bearings.

PLEASURE CRUISING ON THE *BOLDT CANAL* WITH *#13 – THAT* ON THE LEFT

Water inlets, gas intake and water discharge pipes were to be of copper and bronze; water jacket exhaust manifold; double ignition by *Bosch* low-tension magneto with magnetic make-and-break plugs and a secondary system by high-tension coil, distributor and storage battery, including all necessary wiring encased in fiber bushed, brass tubing. Lubrication was to be by *Pedersen* mechanical force-feed oilers, feeding to the cylinders, with a force-feed lubrication by gear-pumps to the main bearings and connecting rods.

The reverse gear was to be of *Jencick* design, to be made of vanadium steel and bronze and mounted on *Hess-Bright* ball-bearings; *Jencick* starting device, consisting of sprockets, nickel steel chain and steel starting handle with bronze sleeve, starting handle with bronze sleeve, starting handle aft of engine bulkhead with automatic release. To start the *Jencick* engine it was cranked from the operators cockpit by means of a shaft with sprockets and chains.

THAT   was #13 of the 20 identical boats built at the *Leyare Boat Works*, of Ogdensburg, New York for the *Thousand Islands Yacht Club* members. *George C. Boldt* became the owner of #13, a number, which he had a fondness for and no superstitions of. In fact he used or chose everything he could around the number 13, the name thirteen, or any creative way 13 could be applied. The twenty boats that were built were referred to as the *"Number"* boats, so called because each had a large black number painted on the hull. *That* or #13 was not listed on the inventory of watercraft owned by *Mr. Boldt* and inventoried on July 14, 1917 at the *Boldt Yacht House* after his death.

It is believed that both the boats *That* and *This Mr. Boldt* owned were acquired by *Mr. Edward J. Noble* when he became the sole owner of almost all of the former *George C. Boldt* estate in 1925. *Mr. Noble* renamed #13 - *That* and called it the *June*. Both the motor boats *(#3 and #13)* were in storage for about 20 years and eventually *#13 - That - June* - was sold by *Mr. Noble's* grandson, *Mr. Noble Smith*, to *Mr. Robert O. Cox* of Grindstone Island, Clayton, New York and Ft. Lauderdale, Florida. The boat *"was in gutted, stripped condition with some of the parts missing."* *Mr. Cox* paid about $12,000.00 for it when he acquired it around 1985. He renamed the boat to *That* the name *George C. Boldt* had originally given it. The registration number is 7G932.

As former Mayor of Ft. Lauderdale and owner of *The Lauderdale Marina, Mr. Cox* had *"rebuilt it complete, with total refinishing, reinstallation of the engine, new fuel tank, new wiring and a whole great big long list of detail improvements including plating of all the hardware."* During the spring of 1987 *Mr. Cox* put *That* up for sale. The asking price was $30,000.00. When a buyer could not be found, he donated the boat to *The Shipyard Museum*, (now known as the *Antique Boat Museum*), where it was on display in their hall of launches. <u>*Mr. Cox's* generous contribution is greatly appreciated</u>! The boat *That* - #13 is now on loan to *The Thousand Islands Bridge Authority* who owns the *Boldt Yacht House* and is on public display.

NUMBER 3 OF THE *ONE DESIGN CLASS* WAS OWNED BY *GEORGE C. BOLDT.* HE CALLED THE BOAT *"THIS."* THE PEOPLE ABOARD ARE UNDENTIFIED

THIS was the third *"One-Design Class"* boat built at the *Leyare Boat Works* in Ogdensburg, New York. It was #3 of the 20 numbered boats built and *George C. Boldt* called it *This*. As mentioned before, it is believed that it was acquired by *Mr. Edward J. Noble* when he became the sole owner of almost all of the former *George C. Boldt* estate in 1925. *Mr. Noble* renamed #3 - *This* - and called it *The Tweet*. It was *"modernized"* in the 1930's into the newly popular double cockpit configuration, its long deck being shortened and the engine located further aft.

Like the other *"Number"* boat that *George C. Boldt* owned *This* - #3 - was in storage for about 20 years and eventually it was sold by *Mr. Noble's* grandson, *Mr. Noble Smith*, to *Mr. James P. Lewis* of Bartlett Point, Clayton, New York and Vero Beach, Florida. The boat was renamed and called *Yesterday*.

Mr. Lewis and his wife *Lorraine E. "Tony" Lewis* were long time antique boat fans whose boats have won innumerable awards all over the eastern parts of the *United States*. One such award was when they won the *Classic Boat of the Year* award at Alexandria Bay, New York's *Vintage Boat Show* in July, 1987. In July of 1990, they donated this fine craft to the *Antique Boat Museum* of Clayton, New York. Their generous contribution is greatly appreciated! Currently the #3 - *This* is on loan to the *Thousand Islands Bridge Authority* and is on public display at the *Boldt Yacht House* on Fern Island off Wellesley Island.

THE *"NUMBERED"* BOATS RACING IN FRONT OF THE VILLAGE OF ALEXANDRIA BAY

WATCHING THE BOAT RACES ON THE ST. LAWRENCE RIVER

TWO VIEWS OF THE 28 FOOT *"NUMBERED BOAT" THIS* IN SEPTEMBER, 1986 AT THE NIAGARA FRONTIER CHAPTER OF *THE ANTIQUE & CLASSIC BOAT SOCIETY'S* 9TH ANNIVERSARY BOAT SHOW HELD AT *THE BUFFALO LAUNCH CLUB* ON GRAND ISLAND, NEW YORK. ITS' OWNER, *MR. JAMES P. LEWIS* RECEIVED *THE BUFFALO LAUNCH CLUB* AWARD AT THAT TIME.

TIA JUANA - was 30 feet over all and had a 5-foot beam. It was powered by a 25-horse power *Fairbanks Smalley* engine. Her speed was 17 miles per hour. The *Tia Juana* was used considerably by *Mr. Boldt's* son, *George C. Boldt Jr.*, when he was at the Thousand Islands.

GEORGE CHARLES BOLDT JR.

FEBRUARY 4, 1879 TO JANUARY 26, 1958 – 78 YEARS

Cruising the Thousand Islands was a boyhood wonderland for young *George C. Boldt Jr.* in his 30-foot motor boat *Tia Juana*. Young *George* was as passionate about the St. Lawrence River as were his parents and younger sister *Louise Clover*. The area became a lifetime place for him to explore and enjoy with his friends and family.

George Charles Boldt Jr. was not as ambitious as his father, but worked with him in the hotel business after he graduated from *Cornell University* in 1905. Young George was a very shy and modest person who had no lofty goals or drive to achieve great fame or fortune. His father left him a handsome endowment that enabled him to retire early and travel the world. He was divorced from his wife *Estelle Savin* in 1927. They had been married 22 years and had two daughters, which each one took to raise.

TOZER - was a 22-footer with a 5-foot beam. It had a 6-horse power *Barker* engine, which gave the *Tozer* a speed of about 10 miles per hour. One article listed the spelling as "*Towser.*"

TROUBLER – no data available yet

TURTLE * - Part of the working fleet was the flat scow named *Turtle*. It was 40 feet long and had an 18 foot beam. It was built in 1906 with a 45-ton capacity. It was appraised on July 14, 1917 for $200.00 and was stated that it required repairs.

ABOVE IS *CHARLES THOMPSON* IN *GEORGE C. BOLDT'S* SKIFF #5. BEHIND HIM IS THE ICE HOUSE AT *MR. BOLDT'S* WELLESLEY ISLAND ESTATE.

According to the appraisal done by *Mr. James H. Hutchinson* on July 14, 1917, there were 19 skiffs at the *George C. Boldt Yacht House* on Fern Island. All were 18 feet long. Above is *Mr. Charles Thompson* in skiff #5. *Mr. Thompson* was a college-educated engineer in charge of the installation and operation of electricity for *George C. Boldt's* estate at the Thousand Islands.

Included in the inventory done on July 14, 1917 appraisal were 7 punts, flat bottom rowboats built around 1912. Three of these punts were entirely out of repair, and all appraised at $150.00. One canoe was part of the collection of watercraft at the *Boldt Yacht House* during the appraisal. Built in 1905 this small canoe was valued at $20.00 in 1917.

The July 14, 1917 appraisal done by *Mr. James H. Hutchinson* also listed some unnamed watercraft owned by *George C. Boldt*. There were 19 skiffs, 18 feet long, made of cedar, over all, and built in 1907. They were valued at $30.00 each. Two unnamed dump scows were also included. They were 50 feet long and had 12-foot beams. Their capacity was 125 cubic yards and were built in 1898. By 1917 they were badly out of repair and valued at $200.00 each.

EVARD WAGONER IN FRONT OF *GEORGE C. BOLDT'S "FRONT FARM"*

GEORGE CHARLES BOLDT SR..

LOUISE AUGUSTA KEHRER BOLDT

April 25, 1851 to December 5, 1916 – 65 years

1862 to January 7, 1904 – 42 years

George C. Boldt Sr. <u>was an amazing man who did amazing things in an amazing way</u>! From humble beginnings on the *Isle of Rugen* in the Baltic Sea, he came alone to America in his mid-teens during the 1860's. Courtesy, ambition, and kindness were his greatest assets. He had a servants heart ……… a willingness to go above and beyond what was expected of him…… and as such he rose to become *"The father of the modern American hotel."* His methods and vision were greatly admired by his peers and his thousands of employee's loyalty never diminished. *Mr. Boldt's* wealth was not merely dollars, but a compassionate concern for people to have jobs. The vastness of his estate attests to that fact. In a letter inviting a friend to his Wellesley Island home in the Thousand Islands he said *"this is where you will see the real man."* It was also said, *"he would rather wear out then rust out."* He was warned by doctors to take it easy, but ignored their advice and continued to work right up to the end. He died in his apartment at the *Waldorf-Astoria Hotel* in New York City of heart failure.

George C. Boldt's love for the Thousand Islands was bigger than all the islands put together! He spent every available moment of his life from that Sunday July 23, 1893 when he first went to Alexandria Bay, to his dying day, with the St. Lawrence River in the fore front of his heart. His love for humanity and nature was also limitless. The life of *George C. Boldt* still impacts society today by the many customs and methods he introduced for the betterment of the hotel industry. As a result of this, those ways and means he instilled to his employees has given to the general public at large much pleasure and enjoyment. We today are the beneficiaries of his kindness and courtesy.

Louise Augusta Kehrer Boldt was indeed a remarkable woman! Her devotion to her husband and two children was unblemished. She worked by her husband's side and encouraged him in every endeavor he undertook. *Louise Boldt* and her husband knew the psychology of the human mind and met the needs of their patrons far and above their expectations. She added the feminine touch to enhance the hotels her husband owned or managed, and gave to the general public a comfort of being *"at home."* A lifetime of frail health never diminished her love, support, and respect for her husband, and children. Her admiration for the Thousand Islands was one of deep enjoyment and pleasure. She died at her home in New York City on January 7, 1904 of heart failure and is buried along side her husband at *Woodlawn Cemetery* in Manhatten.

A Memory   The following tribute appeared in *The Sun Dial*, a feature column on the editorial page of *The Evening Sun* newspaper. *"George C. Boldt* is dead and there are many to pay tribute; but we have our own memory of the man. It is a memory confused with the adventure of a foolhardy boy in a leaky sailboat with a wild bluster of wind and a certain tumult of waters.

"There was a storm from the northeast and the bosom of the broad St. Lawrence River was heaving in majestic anger. The boy was aboard in his leaky boat, very much excited to be out in such a wind – (his seamanship was still a matter for parental regulation and general doubt) – but on the whole rather enjoying the show. Suddenly the boat staggered headfirst into a small hillock of water and came up half drowned. The navigator hauled about and put for home. But the wind smote him and sent him sliding helplessly into the shelter of a stranger's pier.

"It was raining torrents and a black dust had fallen upon the troubled waters. The boy clung desperately to the side of the pier, meanwhile trying to unstep his mast and furl his flapping sail. Then a man came out of the dark and said that all shipwrecked mariners were his guests, and would the boy stay for dinner?

"Forthwith the world came to rights. The youthful adventurer was escorted into the house, was outfitted with sweaters and other extemporized raiment, and went down to dinner feeling like a character out of some thrilling novel of the sea. There were a dozen people seated at the table, all in evening dress and very brilliant. But the boy had donned a high wing collar, which despite the fact that it was several sizes to large for him, nevertheless established him as one inured to the niceties of civilization so that he soon became one of that pleasant company.

"And after a dinner that was like a romance in half a dozen chapters, the boy was sent home in one of his host's stately motor craft – with the chastened sailboat in tow. And the man who made guests of shipwrecked mariners stood on the pier in the rain and waved his hand to the boy.

"The writer of this paragraph was that boy and *George Boldt* was that man. And it is entirely human and sad, and regrettable that we have never been able to thank him.

<u>**NOT THE END**</u> – <u>**by any means**</u>! There is much more to tell about the *Boldt Yacht House* and the history of the *Boldt* family's boats and will be included on future revised publications.

ACKNOWLEDGEMENTS   The information obtained for this *Boldt Yacht House* publication was from many, many sources
PEOPLE   listed below. *MUCH THANKS* is due to the people, places and publications for their kind contributions.

CLOVER BOLDT BAIRD - Alexandria Bay, New York and Delray Beach, Florida
LARRY BALCOLM – Clayton, New York
FRED BEACH - Alexandria Bay, and Bronxville, New York
JAMES and **ERICA BIALY** – Snyder, New York
MARC J. BOYER – Ogdensburg, New York
LES and **VERDA CORBIN** - Clayton, New York
TED and **MARY CORNELL** - Shortsville, New York
ROBERT COX – Clayton, New York and Ft. Lauderdale, Florida
KATHY and **DUDLEY DANIELSON** - Clayton, New York
NANCY E. and **WILLIAM DIXON III** - Clayton, New York
WINSTON DOBBINS - Alexandria Bay and Lyons, New York
DALE FIKES - Philadelphia, New York
ELEANOR and **WILLIAM FORREST** - Alexandria Bay and Syracuse, New York
RICHARD GARITY - Tonawanda, New York
KURT HASSELBALCH – Cambridge, Massachusetts
DONALD "MOE" HUNT – Clayton and Watertown, New York
EDWIN LEVICK - New York, New York
JAMES and **LORRAINE (Toni) LEWIS** - Clayton, New York and Vero Beach, Florida
LINDA M. LUCAS - (my wife) HOME *"The Beach House"* – Cheektowaga, New York
RICHARD and **ISOBEL McALLISTER** - Alexandria Bay, New York
HAZEL SIMPSON McMANE - Alexandria Bay, New York
A. C. MCINTYRE - photographer
ANDREW McNALLY III - Alexandria Bay, New York and Chicago, Illinois
ANDREW (SANDY) and **JEANINE McNALLY IV** – Chicago, Illinois
EDWARD (TED) and **MARGARET (PEGGY) McNALLY** - Alexandria Bay, NY and Chicago, Ill.
ALEXANDER MEAKIN - Alexandria Bay, New York and Cleveland, Ohio
TOM, DORIS and **LAWRIE ANN NULTON** - Clayton, New York and Hot Bottom, Pennsylvania
JANE R. PENVOSE - Tonawanda, New York
EMMA PERRY - MICHAEL PERRY– Fort Pierce, Florida
WINDSOR and **KAY PRICE** - Fineview , New York
DONALD G. PRICE – Clayton, New York
DAVID PUTNAM - Alexandria Bay, New York
BETTY JANE McNALLY RAVENEL
DAVE ROGERS – Alexandria Bay, New York
LAWRENCE ROY - Alexandria Bay, New York
SHANE SANFORD – Alexandria Bay, New York
PATRICK J. SIMPSON - Alexandria Bay, New York
JEANNE ROY SNOW - Alexandria Bay, New York

DAVID R. STITH - Cinnaminson, New Jersey
JOHN SUMMERS – Clayton, New York
ROBERT B. WAGONER, SR. - Alexandria Bay, New York and Scottsdale, Arizona
HOWARD, DAVID and **JUDY WILLIAMS** - Lansdowne, Ontario, Canada

ACKNOWLEDGEMENT - PLACES

ANTIQUE BOAT MUSEUM - Clayton, New York
BOLDT CASTLE - HEART ISLAND - Alexandria Bay, New York
BOLDT YACHT HOUSE - Alexandria Bay, New York
BUFFALO PUBLIC LIBRARY - Buffalo, New York
CORBIN'S RIVER HERITAGE - Clayton, New York
CORNELL UNIVERSITY - Ithaca, New York
GRAHAM THOMPSON MEMORIAL MUSEUM - Alexandria Bay, New York
HART NAUTICAL COLLECTIONS - MIT Museum – Cambridge, Massachusetts
HERRESHOFF MARINE MUSEUM – Bristol, Rhode Island
HOLLAND MEMORIAL LIBRARY - Alexandria Bay, New York
HUNT'S DIVE SHOP – Clayton and Waterown, New York
JEFFERSON COUNTY CLERK'S OFFICE - Watertown, New York
JEFFERSON COUNTY HISTORICAL SOCIETY - Watertown, New York
OGDENSBURG PUBLIC LIBRARY - Ogdensburg, New York
ROGER'S MARINE - Alexandria Bay, New York
ST. LAWRENCE RESTORATION – Clayton, New York
SYRACUSE UNIVERSITY - Syracuse, New York
THOUSAND ISLANDS BRIDGE AUTHORITY - Alexandria Bay, New York

BIBLIOGRAPHY

ACKNOWLEDGEMENTS
PUBLICATIONS

Gratitude is extended to those authors, editors and publishers for their courtesy in granting copyright permission to *Research Review Publications*. **MUCH THANKS TO ALL!**

ALEXANDRIA BAY WHERE THE THOUSAND ISLANDS ARE - by Nannette Lincoln
DAILY ON THE ST. LAWRENCE - newspaper - Clayton, New York
HERRESHOFF SAILBOATS - Gregory O. Jones
LLOYD'S REGISTER OF AMERICAN YACHTS
NEW YORK TIMES newspaper - New York, New York
NEW YORK WORLD newspaper – New York, New York
MOTORBOAT MAGAZINE
MUNSEY MAGAZINE – New York, New York
PICTORIAL HISTORY of the THOUSAND ISLANDS - Adrian G. Ten Cate, Editor –
                                                                  Besancourt Publishers
PLEASURE YACHTS OF THE THOUSAND ISLANDS - by Gilbert Mercier

SANTWAY PHOTO-CRAFT COMPANY, INC., Watertown, New York
SYRACUSE SUNDAY HERALD newspaper - Syracuse, New York
THE EVENING NEWS newspaper – North Tonawanda, New York
THE GOLDEN AGE OF THE THOUSAND ISLANDS - by Laurie Ann Nulton
THE GROWTH OF A CENTURY - by John A. Haddock - 1894 - published by Sherman & Co.
THE POST-STANDARD newspaper - Syracuse, New York
THE RUDDER MAGAZINE
THE VISGER'S WORLD - by Les and Verda Corbin
THOUSAND ISLANDS AND THE RIVER ST. LAWRENCE - by James Bayne Company
THOUSAND ISLAND NEWS - Alexandria Bay, New York
THOUSAND ISLANDS SUN - newspaper - Alexandria Bay, New York
TOWN & COUNTRY MAGAZINE - New York, New York
WATERTOWN DAILY TIMES - newspaper - Watertown, New York

Other books produced by the author and about *George C. Boldt* are:

BOLDT CASTLE - HEART ISLAND- (ISBN 1-887287-00-0) now in its' 10th printing and introduced to the public in 1992. It tells of this historic place from 1871 to the present, and the people behind it, both past and present owners. The focus is on the *George C. Boldt* family and their contribution to the place. There are 101 pictures, maps, illustrations included in this 85 page book. *Boldt Castle* opened as a tourist attraction in 1918 and over 200,000 people visit it each year from mid-May to mid-October. *The Thousand Islands Bridge Authority* now owns and operates *Boldt Castle* and has spent over $16 million in restoring the structure since 1977.

BOLDT'S BOATS - (ISBN 1-8877287-01-9) publication is **no longer in print**. The book had 53 pictures and was 62 pages long. It was 7" by 8 & 1/2" in size and introduced to the public in 1993. It had been revised and reprinted three times. In 2006 it was revised and the title changed to *Boldt Yacht House*.

THE BELLEVUE-STRATFORD HOTEL - (ISBN 1-887287-02-7) was done in celebration of this landmark buildings 90th anniversary in 1994. This book tells the early days of Mr. *Boldt*'s life, and his rise to fame in the hotel business. There were 65 photographs and was 62 pages in length. *THE BELLEVUE-STRATFORD HOTEL* **book is out of print**. *The Park Hyatt* in the *Bellevue Building* operates this "*Grand Dame of Broad Street*" which opened on September 20, 1904.

THE WALDORF HOTEL - (ISBN 1-887287-03-5) tells the history of this unique place and its master proprietor *George C. Boldt*. He took the management position when the building was just an idea and under his guidance and leadership it became world renowned for it's lavish appointments, fine cuisine, and superb service. From the time of its conception in 1890 to the early days of 1897, this book gives the historical account of a great enterprise and the guiding genius who brought it to life. This 66 page book contains 24 black and white photographs and 1 colored painting of the hotel on the front cover. It is 7" by 8 & 1/2" in size. The *Astoria Hotel* was added to the *Waldorf Hotel* in 1897 and both were under *Mr. Boldt's* control. Both were torn down in 1929 and **the Empire State Building is now on that site**. *The Waldorf=Astoria Hotel* in New York City now was built in 1931 and at 301 Park Avenue. This book was introduced to the public in 1997.

THE THOUSAND ISLANDS CLUB – (ISBN 1-887287-04-3) book gives the history of this organization and place from its organization in 1894 to the present time. *George C. Boldt*, builder of world famous *Boldt Castle,* played a major role in the promotion and establishment of *The Thousand Island Club* at Alexandria Bay, New York. This book has 50 pictures, 2 in color, 48 in black and white, and is 61 pages long. It is 7" by 8 and 1/2" in size, and was introduced to the public in the spring of 2005.